Twelve Seasons

... Under the Florida Sun

Chef Doug Janousek, editor

Chef Anne Sears Mooney, copy editor

Glenn Porter, proofreader

Published by Home Cookin' LLC
www.home-cookin.net

Bloomington, IN   Milton Keynes, UK

AuthorHouse™
1663 Liberty Drive, Suite 200
Bloomington, IN 47403
www.authorhouse.com
Phone: 1-800-839-8640

AuthorHouse™ UK Ltd.
500 Avebury Boulevard
Central Milton Keynes, MK9 2BE
www.authorhouse.co.uk
Phone: 08001974150

First published by AuthorHouse 11/21/2006

ISBN: 978-1-4259-7871-6 (sc)

Library of Congress Control Number: 2006910048

Printed in the United States of America
Bloomington, Indiana

This book is printed on acid-free paper.

Dedication

This book is for everyone who knows that food nourishes more than just the body. And to my Mom, Marge Janousek, who taught me that no one should leave the table hungry.

Table of Contents

Preface

Cooking is a labor of creativity and love and passion. So too is writing.

This book was born of a union of those two seemingly disparate pursuits.

Believe it or not, there are many similarities between the two: Both require attention to detail, organization and creativity; both require a certain amount of technical skill, patience and the ability to think outside of the recipe box; and finally, the rewards for both endeavors begin with the satisfaction of knowing you have touched someone on an intimate and sensual level. What can be more profound than touching someone's heart by evoking something in them?

Food and the power of words have much in common for they both can nourish the soul.

Since becoming a personal chef I've met up with others of a similar mindset who see their cooking as more than a 9-to-5 or 3-to-midnight vocation. They want to make a difference and touch the people they cook for.

One of my former instructors at the Orlando Culinary Academy, Chef Dale Pyle, who is also a personal chef, sent out an e-mail one day early in 2006 to a bunch of personal chefs in the area asking them if they were interested in forming a local networking group. That first meeting about 12 or 13 of us gathered to talk about what we do and how we do it.

The group meets sporadically as schedules allow with as few as three sometimes getting together to chat and share a meal.

From these chats was born the idea for a cookbook, this cookbook.

Chefs are a varied lot – varied backgrounds, varied styles, varied goals. The one thing we all share is a passion for cooking and preparing good food.

It occurred to me that it would be interesting if we could pool our passions and create something unique … 12 menus, loosely based on a monthly seasonal cycle.

I approached a number of the chefs both within and outside our little networking group and made the pitch for this project. Seven of my colleagues bit and joined forces with me, including two of my former instructors at OCA and another chef who is also a writer.

Next I reached out to a former employee/co-worker and current friend who is an artist and writer to see about illustrating this project and suddenly, like a Sunday night potluck, **12 Seasons Under the Florida Sun** was born.

This whole project has been a learning experience for everyone I think. I know I've learned a lot. For some of the chefs it was their first foray into publishing and everyone's motivations for participating were as varied and personal as the individuals themselves.

For some it was all about marketing themselves; for others it was the chance to be in print; for still others it was something fun to do; for all of us it was intensely rewarding to put in the time and effort to create these menus for our readers and perhaps even potential clients.

As a chef, it has been inspiring and interesting to get an inside look into other chefs' heads to find out how they cook, how they prepare a menu and how they express themselves through food. As a writer and editor, it has been a challenge to bring these varied ingredients together into a cohesive book, while maintaining each chef's voice and vision.

In the end, I think we've succeeded in producing 12 tasty menus ranging from fancy and formal to fabulous and family style.

I hope you enjoy it.

See you in the kitchen!

– Doug Janousek
Orlando, Florida
2006

Acknowledgments

This book wouldn't have been possible without the assistance and patience of each of the chefs who contributed.

My great thanks goes to Chef Anne Sears Mooney for her help in editing this project. Her support and expertise helped me on many levels.

Equal thanks go to the other contributing chefs – Christian Markussen, Angelo Bersani, Mary Sue Brannon, Marla Zell, Dale Pyle and Taty Ramirez.

Many thanks also go to my good friend Anne Jenkins who illustrated the book, including the cover. Her contributions far exceed the paintings that grace these pages.

Thanks go to my friend and former boss, Elaine Heit, who provided words of wisdom and more than a little technical support to get this project going when it was just an idea.

I must also acknowledge my clients, who put up with me talking about this project, some of whom may recognize some of the dishes on my menus.

Many thanks also go to my partner, Glenn, who lent his proofing talents to this project, not to mention his patience and support as it went together. His tasting notes as I tested recipes were invaluable. He is my strictest critic and my biggest fan.

I want to thank all of my friends, colleagues and assorted strangers who listened to me go on and on about "my cookbook project" over the years, up to and including the actual production of this one. Your insights along the way have been more help than you know.

And last, but far from least, I want to thank you, the readers (and eaters!), for buying this book and enjoying the recipes within – without your support we'd all be eating alone.

– Chef Doug Janousek

Introduction

Personal chefing by its very nature is hard to define. Personal chefs are even harder to pigeonhole. The service we provide is as varied as each individual chef and his or her clients.

Therefore it is impossible to label personal chefs with any degree of accuracy. And believe me, in our label-conscious society people will always try. While some people in the industry might try to nail it down and own the term, the chefs in the following pages are happy to revel in their individuality and to keep their services personal while sharing their avocation as chefs: We cook for the love of it.

Our backgrounds are varied – culinary schools, college trained, restaurant kitchen trained ... some of us have done nothing else, some of us are career changers ... but all of us share the desire to prepare food for the body and to nourish the soul – our own as well as our clients.

Some of us prepare a week's worth of meals in a single day or two to be used by our clients whenever they want. Some of us cook a daily meal for each client. Some just do dinner parties for two or more; some prefer to do interactive events with their clients.

Speaking of our clients, each one has something different in mind when they call one of us to talk about service, special dietary needs, special events...

What follows is just a glimpse into what a personal chef can do for you.

The menu in each chapter was personally prepared by each chef. They chose their month, their theme and their recipes. Each of us has tried to explain the inspiration that went into that menu and you'll see that each chef approached their chapter in a unique and personal way.

We hope you enjoy the next year of meals. Feel free to drop any of us a note if you have any questions, comments or concerns.

And remember: It's just food! Have fun!

January

No matter how crazy you were on New Year's Eve, the first day of the new year always seems to call for a little class. That's one reason why it's best to party at someone else's house on December 31st. That way, come January 1, you can deal with your hangover without having to wade through a living room full of confetti and paper streamers and a kitchen full of crusted party dishes and empty beverage bottles.

The first major meal of the year should set the tone for the next 364 days – a relatively healthy counterpoint to all the sugar and sweets you've piled on since Thanksgiving and something that reflects your goals of success and prosperity for the coming year.

A number of traditional dishes that traditionally represent good luck include black-eyed peas and other legumes, usually in combination with ham (as well as other parts of the hog).

Cabbage and other leafy greens like spinach represent paper currency and, therefore, prosperity.

Rice is considered lucky, as is any dish in the shape of a ring, to represent coming full circle – doughnuts for example.

With the year stretching before you, it can't hurt to get as much luck as possible in your corner, right from the start.

– Chef Doug Janousek

Appetizer

Artichoke Shots
A shot glass of pureed Artichoke Heart soup, silken and creamy
to the palate

Salad

Prosperity Spinach Salad
Fresh spinach leaves tossed with bacon and diced boiled eggs, topped
with a tangle of bean sprouts and drizzled with a balsamic vinaigrette

Main Course

Beef Rib Roast
Seared and roasted to pink perfection,
served with Bell Pepper Jus

Baked Squash & Black-Eyed Peas
Acorn squash filled with black-eyed peas in a rich sour cream sauce

Garlic Whipped Potatoes
Yukon Gold potatoes whipped with roasted garlic, butter and cream

Dessert

Doughnut Bread Pudding
Sweet custard-soaked doughnut bits topped with
apricot brandy sauce

Artichoke Shots

4 pounds artichokes (5 or 6 large ones)
3 tablespoons lemon juice
3 cups cold water
2 quarts vegetable stock
1/4 cup olive oil
1 large onion, chopped
2 ribs celery, chopped
3 cloves garlic, minced
1/2 cup white wine
1/2 cup apple juice
1 bay leaf
3 tablespoons sun-dried tomatoes, julienne
Salt and pepper to taste

Method:

Combine two tablespoons lemon juice and the water in a medium mixing bowl.

With a sharp knife (a serrated knife works great) cut off the thick skin at the base of one artichoke. Remove the outer leaves to get to the yellow center. Reserve the leaves. Working quickly, trim to the fuzzy center of the artichoke heart and then using a spoon scrape out the choke. Put the artichoke heart in the lemon-water to keep it from getting dark and repeat with the remaining artichokes.

Put the reserved artichoke leaves in a stockpot with the vegetable stock and bring to a fast boil. Turn down the heat to medium and let simmer for 15 to 20 minutes. Remove the pot from the heat and let it stand for 15 minutes or so to cool and to let the flavors draw through. Strain this stock, pressing the leaves to get as much flavor as possible, then discard the leaves.

Heat 1 tablespoon of olive oil in a large saucepan over medium-high heat. Cook the chopped onion and celery until softened, stirring throughout. Add the garlic and cook another 2 minutes or until softened and aromatic.

Remove artichoke hearts from the lemon water and quickly cut them into thick slices. Add them to the onion and celery, season and cook for about 5 minutes. Add the wine and apple juice and bring to a boil. Reduce the heat to medium and simmer until the liquid is nearly evaporated. Add the bay leaf and the artichoke stock. Bring back to a simmer for about 20 minutes or until the artichoke hearts are tender.

When the chokes are tender, strain the soup into another cooking pot. Discard the bay leaf. In small batches puree the artichokes and vegetables until smooth. Put the pureed vegetables into a saucepan, stir in the remaining olive oil and then add the strained liquid to the puree until you reach the desired consistency (about the thickness of cold heavy cream). Season the soup with salt, pepper and lemon juice to bring out the flavor. Heat gently and serve hot.

To serve, ladle carefully into shot glasses and garnish with a couple pieces of sun-dried tomatoes. For a more traditional presentation, ladle into bowls (about 4).

3

Prosperity Spinach Salad

1 cup balsamic vinegar
1 bunch parsley, chopped
2 tablespoons chopped garlic
1 red onion, chopped fine
1 1/2 cups olive oil
1 tablespoon honey
1 teaspoon Dijon mustard
Salt and pepper to taste

4 cups baby spinach, washed, drained, trimmed
3 boiled eggs, peeled, diced
1/2 pound bacon, fried crisp and crumbled
1 cup bean sprouts

Method:
Combine the dressing ingredients (except oil) in a food processor and process. Continue processing and slowly drizzle in oil.

Divide remaining ingredients into four portions and drizzle with dressing.

Beef Rib Roast

1 tablespoon dried rosemary leaves, crushed
3 garlic cloves, pushed through a press
3/4 teaspoon salt
1/4 teaspoon freshly ground pepper
6- to 7-pound beef rib roast, small end (3 to 4 ribs), well trimmed
2-3 tablespoons olive oil

Method:
Preheat the oven to 450 degrees.

Cut the roast off the bones and reserve the bones. Coat the meat with the olive oil and season with the other ingredients.

With butcher's string, tie roast back onto bones and place in roasting pan, bone side down.

Place the roast in the oven and cook for 20 minutes, then reduce the oven heat to 325 degrees for 14 to 17 minutes per pound, or until the roast's internal temperature reaches 5 degrees less than the desired doneness. The roast will continue to cook after you remove it from the oven and the temperature will rise to the proper temperature.

Bell Pepper Jus

1 pound yellow bell peppers seeded, diced
1 whole onion, small dice
1 teaspoon curry powder
1 teaspoon turmeric powder
1 quart vegetable stock
2 ounces Worcestershire sauce
4 ounces red wine
1/4 teaspoon cayenne pepper
2 tablespoons butter, unsalted
Salt and pepper as needed

Method:

Melt the butter in a medium sauce pan and sweat the onion, pepper and spices over medium heat. Add the stock and Worcestershire and simmer briefly.

Put those ingredients in a blender and blend on high, slowly adding red wine until smooth. Strain back into sauce pan and reduce until it is thick enough to lightly coat the back of the spoon. Season with salt and pepper to taste.

Baked Squash & Black-Eyed Peas

2 acorn squash
1/4 cup butter
1 can black-eyed peas (15 ounce can), drained
1/3 cup sour cream
1/8 teaspoon grated nutmeg
2 tablespoons olive oil
Salt and pepper to taste

Method:

Preheat oven to 350 degrees.

Wash each of the squash, cut in half and remove the seeds. Coat each half with oil and season with salt and pepper. Place cut side down in a shallow baking pan. Add enough water to just barely cover the bottom of the pan. Bake for about 45 minutes or until just barely tender – the squash should not be mushy.

Remove from the oven and turn over, season with salt and pepper if necessary. Fill the squash with the peas, top with butter and return to oven for 20 minutes. Meanwhile in a small sauce pan, warm sour cream with nutmeg, salt and pepper to taste.

When squash are done, remove from the oven, top with sour cream sauce and serve.

Garlic Whipped Potatoes

8 large cloves of garlic, peeled
1/4 cup olive oil
1/4 cup water
Salt and pepper to taste

8 large Yukon Gold Potatoes
1/2 stick butter
1 cup heavy cream
Salt and white pepper to taste.

Method:

Preheat oven to 375 degrees.

In a small baking dish, toss garlic with oil, water, salt and pepper, cover loosely with foil and place in oven for 40 minutes or until aromatic and soft. Remove from oven and let cool slightly, then place in food processor with metal blade and process until smooth.

Meanwhile, in a large saucepan, place cut up potatoes and cover with salted water. Cook potatoes until tender but not mushy. In a small sauce pan, heat cream and butter.

When potatoes are done, drain and place in mixing bowl. Whip on high, adding roasted garlic paste, butter and cream until you reach the desired consistency. Be careful not to over-whip the potatoes. Season with salt and pepper.

Doughnut Bread Pudding

4 glazed doughnuts
1/2 cup dried apricots, chopped
2 eggs
12 ounces heavy cream
2 tablespoons turbinado sugar
1 teaspoon vanilla extract
2 teaspoons ground cinnamon
1/4 teaspoon ground nutmeg
1/2 stick butter

Method:

Preheat the oven to 350 degrees.

Lightly butter four 8-ounce ramekins.

Tear the doughnuts into bite-sized pieces and divide among the ramekins. Divide dried apricots evenly between the ramekins as well.

In a medium mixing bowl whisk together the eggs, cream, sugar and vanilla extract. Stir in cinnamon and nutmeg and pour over doughnut pieces, making sure the pieces are well saturated with the mixture. Let stand for 10 to 15 minutes and add more of the custard mixture if they can take it. These can also be covered and refrigerated over night.

To bake, place the ramekins in a large baking dish and fill the outer pan with water about half way up the side of the ramekins. A small cloth placed in the larger pan under the ramekins helps keep them from sliding around.

Bake for 35 to 40 minutes or until a knife inserted near the center comes out clean. Serve warm.

Apricot Brandy Sauce

1 cup dried apricots
1 cup apple juice
1/2 cup apricot brandy
3 tablespoons butter
1/2 cup brown sugar
2 teaspoons vanilla extract
3 cups heavy cream

Method:

Over night, soak apricots in apple juice and half of apricot brandy.

In a medium saucepan melt butter and brown sugar and allow to just begin to look like caramel. Add vanilla and apricots and soaking liquid and cook until the alcohol is evaporated and the mixture is syrupy. Turn down heat and slowly mix in heavy cream so that the sauce is smooth and silky. It should be slightly thicker than cold, heavy cream. Use the remaining cream to adjust the consistency of the sauce. Just before serving, stir in the last of the brandy.

About the chef ... Doug Janousek

I have been cooking since I was a youngster, with Mom as my first and in many ways best teacher. She taught me the importance of making sure no one leaves the table hungry, which means that the food needs not only to look good and smell good, but to taste good, too.

I was also writing at a fairly young age... I tried to start a student newspaper when I was a fifth-grader.

Since then I have expanded my experiences by being a working journalist for nearly 25 years, including the last several years as a freelance food/recipes columnist.

I almost went to culinary school right out of high school, but was talked out of it by a cranky steakhouse chef.

So, instead I went to college and earned my bachelor of science in Journalism and English with a minor in political science, graduating cum laude in December 1984.

My journalism career has taken me all around the United States, from Florida to Alaska and most of the points in between. I even spent some time working in the Caribbean. All the while I was writing and editing newspapers, I was also cooking for friends and family and soaking up the local food culture.

In 2004 I arranged my life so that I could change careers and attend the Le Cordon Bleu program at Orlando Culinary Academy. I arrived in Orlando from Alaska in November of that year and never looked back.

At school I learned the classic French techniques to go with the recipes I have been honing over the years. My personal style of cooking is to blend the tastes of where I've been to make a tasty meal. I use the freshest ingredients possible and strive to make my meals wholesome, filling and flavorful.

I believe you can eat healthy and still have it taste good; that lower carbs, low sodium or any other special diet doesn't mean you have to sacrifice flavor.

Cooking and writing have always been my passions and education and experience have provided me with a means to combine and share those passions with others.

In 2006 I launched my personal chefing business, Home Cookin' LLC and I continue to look forward.

HOME COOKIN' L.L.C

... A personal chef service

www.home-cookin.net

Chef Doug Janousek is a December 2005 summa cum laude graduate of Orlando Culinary Academy. He holds an associate's degree in applied science, Le Cordon Bleu Culinary Arts and a bachelor of science degree in Journalism and English.

Chef Doug's dinner party clients have included the Austrian Consulate in Orlando as well as a number of private clients.

He has also volunteered his time to cook for the Ronald McDonald House in Orlando and is included in their fund-raising cookbook. He also prepares daily and weekly meals for his regular clients.

Home Cookin' LLC is a Florida limited liability corporation fully licensed and insured to do business in Orlando and the surrounding areas.

Chef Doug is a member of the Central Florida Chapter of the American Culinary Federation and can be contacted via his Web site: djanousek@home-cookin.net.

February

"In general, I think, human beings are happiest at table when they are very young, very much in love or very alone."

– M.F.K. Fisher (1908-1992),
"An Alphabet for Gourmets" (1949)

February is probably my favorite month. Winter is winding down and Spring is just around the corner.

It is during this time that the first fruits of the season start becoming available – citrus.

Citrus gives food a vibrant pop and reminds us of summer days yet to come – beaches and lazy vacation days.

– Chef Christian Markussen

Appetizer
Seared Sea Scallops with Lemon Risotto

Soup
Coconut Curry Soup

Main Course
*Pork Osso Bucco with Sweet Potato Spaetzle and
a Maple-Vinegar Reduction*

Dessert
Tangelo-Ginger Granite with Berry Consommé

Seared Sea Scallops

12 large sea scallops (U-10), rinsed
Olive oil, as needed
Kosher salt and fresh ground black pepper to taste

Method:

Over high heat, quickly sauté scallops in olive oil until browned on one side, then turn and cook the other side until just opaque in the center.

Four servings of three scallops each.

Lemon Risotto

6 cups chicken stock
3 1/2 tablespoons butter
1 1/2 tablespoons extra virgin olive oil
2 shallots, minced
2 cups Arborio rice
1/4 cup Riesling wine
1 cup freshly grated Parmesan cheese
2 tablespoons parsley, minced
1 tablespoon cilantro, minced
2 tablespoons Meyer lemon juice, freshly squeezed
4 tablespoons finely grated lemon zest

Method:

In a saucepan, bring the stock to a simmer; reduce heat and cover to keep warm.

In another saucepan on medium heat, melt half of the butter with the oil and sauté shallots until translucent. Add rice and stir for about one minute. Add the wine and continue to stir until wine is almost all absorbed.

Add the hot stock, one-fourth at a time, stirring constantly until the rice is creamy and al dente and most of the liquid has been absorbed.

Add the cheese and the other half of the butter and stir to incorporate. Then add herbs, lemon juice and lemon zest. Season to taste with salt and pepper.

Serve immediately with the seared scallops.

Four servings.

Coconut Curry Soup

1 can (14-ounce) coconut milk
1/4 cup palm sugar
1 1/2 stalks lemongrass, finely chopped
1/4 cup Asian fish sauce
2 garlic cloves, minced
1/2-inch piece ginger, minced
1 tablespoon red curry paste
2 cups fish or shrimp stock
1/4 cup Canola oil
¾ pound shrimp, peeled and deveined
1 tablespoon (or to taste) Thai basil, leaves only
Juice of one lime
Kosher salt and pepper to taste

Method:

In a saucepan, sauté garlic and ginger in Canola oil until fragrant, then add the curry paste and sauté until fragrant and slightly colored. Add coconut milk, sugar, lemongrass, fish stock and fish sauce. Bring to a boil. Lower heat to a simmer and reduce by one quarter.

Finish the soup by adding fresh lime juice and shrimp, simmering until shrimp are cooked through, approximately five minutes. Taste and adjust seasonings. Add Thai basil as desired, either in whole leaves or as chiffonade. Makes four servings.

Pork Osso Bucco

4 pork shanks, osso bucco cut
1 cup flour, for dredging
1 tablespoon Kosher salt
1 teaspoon freshly ground black pepper
2 tablespoons vegetable oil
1 quart beef stock

Method:

Preheat oven to 300 degrees.

Season pork with salt and pepper and dredge in flour.

Heat oil in a heavy oven-proof skillet and brown the pork well on all sides.

Remove pork from skillet and keep warm. Add stock to deglaze the pan.

Return pork to pan and bring the liquid to a boil. Cover the skillet and place in the oven for 2 1/2 hours, adding liquid if pan dries out.

Remove when pork is fork tender. Serve with sweet potato spaetzle and maple vinegar reduction. Four servings.

Sweet Potato Spaetzle

3 eggs, beaten
1 tablespoon heavy cream
5 teaspoons butter, melted
1 1/3 cup cooked sweet potato, mashed
1/2 teaspoon Kosher salt
1 1/2 cups flour
2 tablespoons butter
1/4 cup raw sweet potato, minced
1 teaspoon chives, minced
Kosher salt and freshly ground black pepper to taste

Method:

Mix together the eggs, cream, melted butter, salt and mashed sweet potatoes. Add the flour and mix until a dough forms.

Bring a saucepan of salted water to a boil and, using an offset spatula, scrape thin ribbons of dough into boiling water. When the spaetzle floats, remove and shock in an ice water bath.

When chilled, remove spaetzle and pat dry with a paper towel. Heat butter in a sauté pan, add grated sweet potatoes and cook until they soften, add the spaetzle, chives and seasonings. Heat through and serve.

Four servings.

Maple Vinegar Reduction

2 tablespoons butter
1/4 cup shallots, chopped
1/2 teaspoon black pepper
1/4 teaspoon nutmeg, freshly ground
1/3 cup cider vinegar
1/3 cup maple syrup

Method:

Melt butter in medium saucepan over medium-high heat. Add the shallots and sweat.

Add the pepper and nutmeg. Add the vinegar and bring to a boil, then add maple syrup. Return the sauce to a boil and cook until it returns to maple syrup thickness.

Serve with Pork Osso Bucco and Sweet Potato Spaetzle.

Yields two cups.

Tangelo-Ginger Granite

Juice of 2 tangelos
1 1/2 cups granulated sugar
3 cups water
1-inch piece ginger, finely grated
1/2 teaspoon tangelo zest, finely grated

Method:

In a heavy bottomed saucepan, mix the ginger with the water and sugar and gently simmer for two minutes, stirring to make sure all of the sugar dissolves. Do not allow liquid to color. Remove from heat and steep for at least 15 minutes.

Add the citrus juice and zest to the cooled ginger syrup.

Place in a shallow pan and place in the freezer. Freeze until solid, or overnight in a regular freezer.

To serve, use a fork to scrape the surface of the ice to form small flakes.

Makes four servings.

Berry Consommé

1 cup raspberries
2 cups strawberries
1 cup blackberries
1 cup water
1/4 cup corn syrup
1 1/2 tablespoons brandy

Method:

In a medium sauce pan, bring the berries and water to a boil and simmer for 10 minutes.

Strain the mixture through a fine mesh sieve; add the corn syrup and brandy and then chill. Serve with Tangelo-Ginger Granite.

Yields two cups.

About the chef ... Christian Markussen

Chef Christian Markussen has been in the food industry for 16 years. Originally from Northern California, he is a graduate of the California Culinary Academy in San Francisco.

Upon graduation, Chef Markussen worked in Helsinki, Finland, for six months and then in Italian restaurants around the San Francisco Bay area before moving to Florida.

Once in Florida, Chef Markussen worked for Walt Disney World Resorts at restaurants like the Yachtsman Steakhouse, Victoria and Albert's and Jiko...the Cooking Place.

Chef Markussen currently is an instructor at the Orlando Culinary Academy and a personal chef specializing in in-home cooking lessons.

March

You might think it odd to include a Mardi Gras menu for the month of March since Fat Tuesday typically falls during the month of February. However, thanks to an area theme park, Mardi Gras is three months long in Orlando – February, March and April.

As a personal chef serving the Orlando and Central Florida area since 2003, I have been asked to prepare numerous Mardi Gras-themed meals for groups of revelers either on their way to the festivities or for those simply inspired by the season. This menu is a tribute to many such parties.

Ideally, you would invite me to prepare this sumptuous feast for you. However, all of these recipes are easy enough to prepare on your own in their entirety or in part depending on your mood and motivation. They are delicious and fun to eat with family and friends.

One key to this great meal is the quality of the products you use. The freshness of the food you purchase has a direct relationship with the quality of the meal you serve. Talk to your grocer about when his products arrived and where they originated.

While local is best, it is not always possible to get what you need locally. Substitutions for many of the vegetables are recommended if what you find in the store is not up to par.

For example, if you can't find fresh French green beans, you can use regular green beans, asparagus or even broccoli in the almandine recipe. Another tip: prepare the Crème Brûlée and the composed butters early in the day to allow time for proper chilling before serving.

Using quality meat is vital. I am a huge believer that meat should never be frozen. Ask your grocer or butcher for meat that is fresh and never frozen.

For this menu, I suggest Hereford beef, which is known for superior meat quality worldwide. It is available at most high-end meat counters.

Good food nourishes the body and soul. Make sure the ingredients are the best and that the meal is prepared with great love and laughter.

If you have any questions during any part of your preparation, please do not hesitate to contact me.

– Chef Angelo Bersani

Appetizer

Garlic Shrimp Appetizer
Jumbo gulf shrimp prepared with garlic, shallots and white wine
Served with toasted herb garlic rounds

Soup

Vegetarian Gumbo
A twist on an old favorite featuring fresh garden vegetables

Main Course

Filet Mignon with Creole Sauce
Aged Hereford steaks served with a Creole sauce of traditional
seasonings and herbs

Bayou Beans and Rice
Red beans and confetti rice

Sautéed Haricots Verts Almandine
French green beans sautéed in olive oil graced with an herb compound
butter and toasted almonds

Dessert

Crème Brûlée
Traditional French custard

Garlic Shrimp Appetizer

2 tablespoons extra virgin olive oil
3 large garlic cloves, minced
2 tablespoons diced shallots
Salt and pepper
1/2 cup dry white wine
2 tablespoons fresh lemon juice
1 stick of butter, softened
4 teaspoons fresh chopped parsley
4 teaspoons fresh chopped oregano
4 teaspoons fresh chopped basil
4 teaspoons fresh chopped thyme
1 teaspoon cayenne pepper (optional)
3 1/2 pounds colossal size (U-10 or bigger) gulf shrimp, peeled and deveined, with tail on.
1 loaf focaccia bread, sliced and toasted

Method:

To make the compound butter, heat the olive oil over medium heat in a sauté pan. Add garlic and shallots and cook until soft or about two to three minutes.

Add wine and reduce by half.

Add lemon juice and continue to reduce until almost dry.

Remove from heat and transfer to a small bowl. Let cool completely before adding the butter.

When cooled, add the softened butter, fresh herbs and pepper. Blend well. Transfer the butter into a small container and chill until hard. Or, chill butter mixture slightly first, then form into a log about one inch in diameter and roll in plastic wrap for storage. Butter may then be sliced into disks after chilling.

Chef Angelo's note: This can be made in advance to allow flavors to develop. It will keep refrigerated and well wrapped for up to two weeks or frozen for up to two months.

To prepare the shrimp, place the rack in center of oven. Preheat oven to 475 degrees. Place the focaccia on a sheet pan and toast lightly. Set aside. Grease a large jelly roll pan with a small amount of the compound butter. Butterfly the shrimp by laying it flat and, beginning at the larger head end, slice it down the center of the back about three-quarters of the way through, leaving the tail intact. Spread the two sides of the shrimp, pressing to flatten and place it in the pan with the tail up. Cut the compound butter log into disks or scoop about a teaspoon and place on each shrimp.

Mix the remaining wine and lemon juice and pour into the pan. Salt and pepper to taste. Roast shrimp until firm, about 5 minutes. Transfer shrimp to a platter and keep warm.

Strain pan liquids into a small saucepan and reduce on medium high heat until thickened, about two or three minutes. Plate the shrimp, spoon sauce over the top and garnish with remaining herbs. Serve with toasted focaccia.

Vegetarian Gumbo

1 tablespoon vegetable oil
1 tablespoon olive oil
1 large onion, chopped
1 large green bell pepper, seeded and chopped
1 large red bell pepper, seeded and chopped
2 large celery sticks, chopped
1/2 pound fresh okra, cut into rounds
1/2 pound fresh corn, cut from the cob
2 large fresh tomatoes, seeded and chopped
Jalapeno peppers to taste (optional), seeded and chopped
2 cans (14-ounce) vegetable broth
2 cups water
4 ounces butter and 6 ounces all purpose flour for brown roux
1 bay leaf
Creole seasoning

Method:

Make a roux before beginning gumbo by using 4 ounces of butter and 6 ounces of all purpose flour. Melt butter on low heat, then add flour and stir to combine. Continue cooking mixture on low heat until it turns brown, stirring frequently. Remove from heat and let cool.

In an 8-quart saucepan over medium heat, heat vegetable oil. Add onions, bell peppers and celery and sweat the vegetables.

Add broth, water and bay leaf. Bring to simmer.

Add okra and corn and cook until tender.

Add jalapenos and Creole seasonings to taste. Bring back to a simmer, season to taste. Add roux to bring to desired thickness.

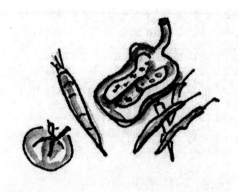

Filet Mignon with Creole Sauce

1 tablespoon butter
1 tablespoon olive oil
1 large garlic clove, minced
1/2 cup chopped onions
1/2 cup chopped green bell pepper
1/2 cup chopped red bell pepper
1/2 cup chopped celery
1 teaspoon paprika
2 teaspoons Creole seasoning
1/2 teaspoon dried thyme
1/2 teaspoon dried oregano
1/2 teaspoon dried basil
1 teaspoon Worcestershire sauce
1 teaspoon hot pepper sauce
1/2 teaspoon fresh ground black pepper
1 can (28-ounce) crushed tomatoes
1 can (14-ounce) of chicken broth
1 tablespoon tomato paste
4 green onions, chopped
1 teaspoon fresh thyme, finely chopped
1 teaspoon fresh oregano, finely chopped
1 teaspoon fresh basil, finely chopped
4 prime cut filet mignon, 10-ounce or larger, seasoned well with salt and pepper
2 tablespoons vegetable oil

Method:

To prepare the Creole sauce heat the butter and oil in a heavy saucepan over medium heat.

Combine the dried seasonings, Worcestershire sauce and hot sauce in a small bowl.

Sauté the garlic, onions, peppers and celery until soft or about two to three minutes. Add the tomatoes and heat through. Add the seasoning mixture and combine.

Add chicken broth and simmer uncovered until most of the liquid cooks away, about 10 to 15 minutes. Stir in the tomato paste and blend well.

Remove from heat and add fresh herbs, green onions and butter, stirring until butter is melted.

To prepare the filet, preheat oven to 400 degrees.
Foil and spray a sheet pan.
In a large heavy skillet, heat the oil over medium high heat. Quickly sear each side of the filets and place on the baking sheet.

Let filets cool completely before roasting. When cooled, roast meat in the oven until it reaches internal temperature of 145 degrees, about 15 to 20 minutes.

Remove from oven and allow meat to stand 5 minutes before plating.

Plate and serve with Creole sauce, garnish with fresh herbs.

Bayou Beans

2 cans (15 ounces) red kidney beans
3 slices bacon
1 large onion, chopped
1 small bell pepper, chopped
1/2 cup chopped green onions
1/2 cup chopped celery
2 tablespoons chopped parsley
1 teaspoon Worcestershire sauce
2 ounces chopped pimento
8 ounces tomato paste
1 cup water
1 bay leaf
1 teaspoon chili powder
Fresh oregano and thyme

Method:

Pour beans with liquid into a bowl.

In a 6-quart saucepan, fry bacon over medium heat until crisp and the fat has rendered.

Remove bacon and crumble into the beans. Reserve fat.

In the same saucepan, add the vegetables and sauté in the bacon drippings until they are softened. Add tomato paste and mix well. Add remaining ingredients, except herbs.

Cover and simmer 30 minutes. Season with salt and pepper to taste.

Add herbs and serve over rice.

Chef Angelo's note: Traditional red beans require soaking dried beans overnight and slow cooking them with a ham bone. This variation captures the flavor of the slow cooked variety by using canned beans and bacon.

Confetti Rice:

2 tablespoons butter
1 cup basmati rice
1/2 cup finely chopped red and green bell pepper
1/2 cup finely chopped onions
1 can chicken broth

Method:

In a 2-quart saucepan, melt butter over medium heat. Sauté the peppers and onions until tender (about 5 minutes).

Add rice and mix with peppers and onions until coated.

Add broth and bring to simmer. Cover and cook until all liquid is absorbed. Serve topped with Bayou Beans.

Haricots Verts Almandine

1 stick of butter, softened
1 large garlic clove, finely chopped
1 small shallot, finely chopped
4 teaspoons fresh thyme, finely chopped
4 teaspoons fresh tarragon, finely chopped
2 tablespoons olive oil, divided
1 tablespoon vegetable oil
1/2 pound French green beans (Haricots Verts), snipped and dried
1/2 cup toasted almonds

Method:

To prepare the compound butter heat 1 tablespoon olive oil over medium heat in a sauté pan.

Add garlic and shallots and cook until soft, 2 to 3 minutes.

Remove from heat and transfer to a small bowl. Let cool completely.

When cooled, add the softened butter, fresh herbs and pepper. Blend well.

Transfer the butter into a small container and chill until hard. Or, chill slightly then form into a log about 1 inch in diameter and roll in plastic wrap. After chilling, slice into disks.

To prepare the haricots verts, cook in boiling salted water for about 4 minutes until they are crisp-tender. Drain and dry.

Heat 1 tablespoon olive and 1 tablespoon vegetable oil in a heavy sauté pan. Add beans and sauté over medium heat until they begin to brown. Be sure to keep them moving.

Remove from heat and place in a wide bowl. Add some compound butter, toasted almonds, salt and pepper.

Toss until almonds and butter are dispersed.

Chef Angelo's note: Haricots verts or French beans are a very thin variety of green bean that is crisp and tender. Don't confuse with the haricot bean, which is a dry bean.

Crème Brûlée

2 cups heavy cream
4 tablespoons sugar
4 extra large or jumbo egg yolks
1 vanilla bean
Boiling water

Method:

To prepare the custard, preheat oven to 300 degrees and place rack in the center of the oven.

Pour cream and sugar into a small saucepan. Slice the vanilla bean down its center then scrape loose the seeds and add seeds and pod to the cream.

Over medium heat, bring cream to a simmer; do not let the mixture boil. Remove from heat.

In a large bowl, whip egg yolks until smooth and light. Remove the vanilla bean husk from the cream.

Slowly add the hot cream to the egg yolks while whisking continuously. Be sure the bowl does not move while you are doing this.

Strain the mixture through a fine sieve into a clean bowl. Divide mixture into four 8-ounce ramekins.

Arrange ramekins in a deep baking pan and place on the middle rack of the oven. Pour boiling water into the pan, about half-way up the sides of the ramekins. Make sure not to get any water in the ramekins. Cover the pan loosely with foil.

The water bath allows the custard to cook in slow gentle heat and prevents curdling and cracking as it bakes.

Bake until custard is just set, but still trembling in the center, about 30 to 35 minutes. Remove ramekins from pan and cool completely on a wire rack.

Cover and refrigerate for at least three hours.

Prepare the topping no more than 30 minutes before serving, otherwise the sugar will melt into the custard and ruin the signature sweet crispy topping. To prepare the topping, sprinkle and evenly disperse 1 teaspoon or so of sugar across the top of the chilled custards. Using a Brûlée torch, heat the sugar on the top of each custard until it begins to brown and bubble, which creates the traditional topping for this dessert. Use quick, small circular motions to avoid burning the custard.

Chill again for at least 15 minutes before serving.

About the chef ... Angelo Bersani

Chef Angelo Bersani is a licensed personal chef who has been serving Orlando and Central Florida since 2003. His emphasis is on the quality and freshness of the meals served. Chef Angelo prepares everything on location and the service is intimate, personal and customized.

Chef Angelo specializes in Mediterranean, North African, American and Latin cuisines. His clients include businesses, private individuals and families.

With more than 20 years experience in entertainment and event management, Chef Angelo also holds both a culinary arts degree from the Florida Culinary Institute in Palm Beach and a bachelor of arts degree in Theatre from Rowan University.

Chef Angelo is a member of the American Culinary Federation and the American Personal Chef Association.

Please contact him for your free, personalized consultation: 407-346-0664 www.angelosprivatedining.com, chef@angelosprivatedining.com

April

No matter what part of the country you live in, April is the epitome of Spring. Even in the sunny South, where seasons sort of run together, our internal calendar triggers something in us, reminding us that despite our city ways we are still tied to Mother Nature and her seasons.

Lengthening days and warming weather lead us to seek out lighter fare as we anticipate the coming heat of summer, which comes sooner to Florida than to many other areas of the country.

April is a good time to look at salads and seafood as part of the lighter cuisine. But since it can still cool down in the evenings, not everything on the menu should be served cold.

A hearty touch balances the lighter fare, like fluffy potato gnocchi to go with tender lamb chops simply braised.

Fresh broccoli barely steamed and drizzled with butter and a hint of garlic finish off the main course.

Ricotta cheesecakes with fruit compote finish the meal on a rich, yet light note.

– Chef Doug Janousek

Appetizer

Squid & Arugula Bites
Seared Squid tossed in a zingy garlic & sesame vinaigrette
served on a bed of Arugula

Soup

Spring Vegetable Potage
A fresh light medley of seasonal vegetables and small shell pasta,
garnished with crispy fried vegetables

Salad

Roasted Beets & Goat Cheese
Golden Beets roasted to sweet tenderness provide earthy contrast to
tangy goat cheese, accented by a citrus and fennel vinaigrette

Main Course

Braised Lamb Chops
Seared and then braised in rich stock
to melt-in-your-mouth tenderness

Polenta Spoon Bread
Topped with roasted tomatoes and mushrooms, these little corn cakes
made with creamy, flavorful polenta are light but filling

Dessert

Ricotta Cheesecakes
Individual cheesecakes topped with fresh fruit compote for a light finish

Squid & Arugula Bites

12 ounces squid tentacles and bodies, cleaned, cut in half horizontally
4 large shallots, peeled and cut into 1/4 inch rings
2 cloves garlic, minced
2 tablespoons olive oil
1 tablespoon sesame oil
2 tablespoons red wine vinegar
2 tablespoons chopped fresh parsley
3 cups loosely packed arugula leaves
Salt and pepper to taste

Method:

Cook the shallots in a small saucepan of boiling water for 2-3 minutes, until just barely tender.

Drain and set aside, covered.

In a sauté pan, heat the olive oil over medium-high heat and sauté the garlic until it just starts to brown, Add the squid and season with salt and pepper. Cook, stirring constantly, for about a minute.

Transfer to a bowl and toss with the shallots. Drizzle with the sesame oil and red wine vinegar and continue to toss, stir in the parsley and adjust seasoning.

Arrange the arugula on salad plates or on a platter, spoon the warm squid salad over the top and enjoy.

Spring Vegetable Potage

1/4 cup olive oil
2 onions, thinly sliced
2 cloves garlic, minced
1 small eggplant, peeled and cubed
2 medium zucchini, sliced
2 yellow squash, sliced
1 bell pepper (any color), seeded and diced
3 stalks celery, sliced
2 carrots, thinly sliced
2 cups mushrooms, sliced
1 pound roma tomatoes, chopped
1 quart chicken stock
2 cups white wine
1 1/2 tablespoons fresh oregano
1 tablespoon fresh cilantro
1/2 teaspoon ground coriander
4 ounces small shell macaroni, cooked al dente, cooled and drained
Salt and pepper to taste

Method:

In a medium stock pot heat the oil and sauté the onion and garlic until the onion is translucent.

Add the carrots, celery, eggplant, zucchini, squash and green pepper and cook over medium heat, stirring constantly, until they just start to brown, about 10 minutes.

Add tomatoes and mushrooms and continue cooking until the tomatoes begin to break down.

Add stock, white wine and herbs.

Bring all of this to a boil, cover and reduce to a simmer for 10 to 12 minutes or until vegetables just start to get tender.

Add macaroni and bring back to a simmer to heat through.

Roasted Beets & Goat Cheese Salad

1 large beet
3 tablespoons olive oil
2 small fennel bulbs, trimmed (discard feathery tops)
1/2 cup minced shallots
2 cloves garlic, minced
1 bay leave
2 sprigs fresh thyme
1 cup apple juice
3 oranges, peeled and sectioned (supremed)
1/4 cup orange juice
2 tablespoons lemon juice
1/4 cup olive oil
6 ounces goat cheese, cut into rounds
4 cups mixed greens
Salt and pepper to taste

Method:

Preheat oven to 400 degrees.

Wash beet thoroughly. Coat with 1 tablespoon olive oil, season with salt and pepper and roast until easily pierced with a fork but not mushy. Remove from oven and let cool.

When the beet is cool, peel and slice it into four equal rounds.

Trim the root ends of the fennel, but don't cut too deeply so the layers stay connected. Cut the fennel into eight wedges.

In a medium saucepan over medium heat, heat two tablespoons olive oil and cook the shallots until softened. Add garlic, bay leaf and thyme. Season with salt and pepper and cook for an additional couple of minutes. Add fennel and enough apple juice to just cover. Bring to a boil, then reduce heat and simmer until the fennel is just tender, about 10 minutes. Remove from heat and let the fennel cool in the cooking liquid.

Whisk together the orange juice, lemon juice and 1/4 cup olive oil and season with salt and pepper to taste. Dress the greens with a few tablespoons of this dressing until the leaves are coated but not drenched.

To make the salad, arrange the beet slices on salad plates with slices of goat cheese and the wedges of fennel, top with a small mound of greens, arrange the orange slices on the plate and dress with more of the citrus dressing.

Braised Lamb Chops

4 double-cut loin lamb chops
2 tablespoons olive oil
1 sprig fresh rosemary
1 large shallot, peeled and minced
1 clove garlic, minced
3/4 cup beef stock
3/4 cup white wine
2 tablespoons butter
Salt and pepper to taste

Method:

Preheat the oven to 375 degrees.

Coat chops with olive oil and season with salt and pepper.

Heat an oven-proof sauté pan over high heat until very hot. Sear the chops on each side (about 4 minutes each side). Add the stock, rosemary, shallot and garlic and braise in the oven for about 10 minutes. Turn the chops and leave in the oven for another 5 minutes.

Remove from the oven and place chops on a warmed plate and cover loosely with foil to keep warm.

Return sauté pan to the stove and bring to a boil, then add wine and simmer until reduced to about a cup of liquid.

Strain into a clean sauce pan and over medium heat swirl in the butter, adjust seasoning and serve over plated chops.

Polenta Spoon Bread

3 cups chicken stock
1 cup cornmeal
1 cup corn kernels
1 cup shredded Parmesan cheese
1 cup heavy cream
3 eggs separated
3 tablespoons butter
1 teaspoon salt

Method:

Preheat oven to 375 degrees.

Heat stock in a medium sauce pan until just about to boil, reduce heat and whisk in cornmeal, stirring constantly until it begins to thicken (three to four minutes).

Remove from heat and add salt, corn kernels, 2 tablespoons butter and cream.

Meanwhile, beat egg yolks and temper with a little bit of the cornmeal mixture then pour into remaining cornmeal mixture, stir in cheese and allow to cool slightly.

Meanwhile, beat egg whites until stiff and fold into cornmeal mixture.

Pour into individual buttered ramekins and bake until puffed and golden (30 to 40 minutes). Serve with additional butter and black pepper.

Ricotta Cheesecakes

6 tablespoons butter
3 large eggs
1/2 teaspoon salt (optional)
2 cups ricotta cheese
2 tablespoons lime zest
3 cups sugar
2 teaspoons nutmeg
8 ounces cream cheese softened
2 teaspoons vanilla
2 tablespoons lime juice
1 tablespoon soy flour
2 tablespoons whole wheat flour

Method:

Preheat oven to 375 degrees. Spray a muffin tin with no-stick spray.
Beat eggs in a mixing bowl until very frothy.
Add ricotta, butter and cream cheese and beat again.
Beat in flour, lime juice, lime zest and sugar. Divide evenly among the muffin cups and dust with nutmeg. Bake for 30 minutes. Remove from oven and let cool. Unmold and serve slightly warm or at room temperature.

Fruit Compote

1/2 cup apple juice
1/2 cup white wine
2 medium peaches, peeled, pitted, chopped
1 medium pear, peeled, cored, chopped
1 medium nectarine, peeled, pitted, chopped
1/2 small pineapple, peeled, cored, chopped
1/2 cup dried cranberries
3 tablespoons sugar
1 teaspoon ground cinnamon
1/2 teaspoon ground nutmeg
Pinch of salt

Method:

Combine ingredients in a medium sauce pan and simmer until the fruit is soft. Serve over ricotta cheesecakes.

Culinary student and chef to be Doug Janousek competes in a cooking competition held at the Orlando Culinary Academy. Students were teamed up with professional chefs to create a meal from "mystery" ingredients. Janousek and his team took second place, netting him a $1,500 scholarship.

About the chef ... Doug Janousek

Culinary school, like most schools, is all about the how – the technique.

The other big questions – who, what, when and where – often are left to answer themselves. The hardest one to answer is the one which dogs us from the time we are children: Why?

Just when we think we have it figured out, the answer changes. Why?

So why does a cook, cook? Why?

To eat of course, to feed one's family, to survive, if you do it for a living, then to make money, pay the bills ... but is there more to it?

I can honestly say it makes me happy to chop vegetables to just the right size, to stir risotto until it is creamy and tender, to roll out and bake loaves of cinnamon-apple-pecan bread (when I worked as a prep cook for a restaurant) and to write and prepare new recipes.

If you're lucky, what you do for a living pleases you the same way.

Nevertheless, when I started culinary school and applied for restaurant jobs and now that I'm in business for myself, the most common question I am asked is, "Why?"

Despite my years of writing and editing, I am often at a loss for words to give a complete answer as to why I changed careers.

Usually when I try to explain, I get a vague look of understanding and a head nodding, but I don't think the words have done it justice.

I mean, where's the glamour and passion in peeling and chopping 20 pounds of onions, 10 pounds of carrots and 10 pounds of celery? What can be so glorious about stirring risotto until your arm aches? (That's the secret to risotto, you know … sweat some onion in some butter, add the uncooked risotto and coat it with the fat, add some white wine and stir until it is absorbed, then start ladling warm stock and stirring until each ladle full is absorbed, add some more until the risotto grains are tender and the liquid is creamy … finish with parmesan, cream, salt and pepper and there you have it. It's all in the arm!)

Where's the joy in coming home from a hard day at work and turning around and spending an hour or two cooking, only to be faced with dishes and clean up afterward?

A lot of that can be chalked up to satisfaction in a job well done, but again, why?

Kitchens are hot. Home or commercial, they are hot – ovens, burners, fryers, grills – in a commercial kitchen the heat is palpable. You step in and feel it in every pore.

Not only that, kitchens require a lot of cleaning, sometimes before you can even get to cooking, not to mention as you go and certainly when you're done.

And they're crazy places. Chaotic. But if you step back out of the way and watch, it is also like a dance as people do their jobs, rushing sometimes from one end of the kitchen to the other, somehow never (well, seldom) crashing into each other.

And they're noisy. Depending on the chef, there's music of some sort blaring, loud on one end, barely heard at the other. Chefs yelling orders (*expediting* they call it), cooks shouting "Heard!" and repeating the orders, servers clamoring for orders, pots and pans banging, the dishwasher singing (they always seem to be singing), the rush of water as the dish machine kicks on, someone laughing … bang, clatter, crash … it is a symphony to accompany the dance.

And did I mention it is hot?

Of course when you dash into the walk-in cooler or freezer for supplies you get respite from that heat, but it is too cold to linger and you have orders to get out anyway.

So it comes back to why?

Why in the world would I give up nearly 25 years of sitting comfortably in front of a computer screen editing and writing 8 to 10 hours a day to spend that same amount of time on my feet cutting and slicing and sautéing and braising and baking and roasting?

Why, indeed.

When I make that perfect, uniform cut; when I get that stainless steel to shine; when I hone my knife to surgical sharpness; when I get that sauce to the right consistency, the right flavor, the right color; when I see someone's face the first time they taste something I've made, the little smile of wonder, the look they give not only to me, but to the plate of food before them, that look of sensual pleasure; when those things happen, each and every time they happen, by themselves and all at once – that's why I do this.

May

May is really the heart of Spring, when the season's bounty is at its best. It isn't quite summer yet, but we know summer isn't far away. Warming days and still-cool nights lend themselves to a light, fresh menu.

When I was growing up in Nebraska, May was my favorite month. The garden was just getting started and by the end of the month (my birthday is at the end of the month!), the first harvests of baby lettuces, and sometimes even radishes and onions if April had been warm enough for Dad to get the garden going, would be ready.

When composing the menu for May, I looked for ingredients that are not only fresh and available, but for ways to prepare them that would be light and refreshing, incorporating as many fresh flavors as possible.

This menu also reflects some of the geographical influences in my life, ranging from Alaska to Florida and the Caribbean, as well as my Le Cordon Bleu training.

Fresh salmon in the starter course, accented by fresh dill, is a nice way to start celebrating the season.

Pea tendrils are a way to get a fabulous early taste of what the garden promises for summer.

Tender veal, fresh asparagus and new red potatoes keep it light.

Finally, stuffed poached pears provide a sweet, spicy ending to the meal with a pleasant surprise of mascarpone cheese inside.

See you in the kitchen!

– Chef Doug Janousek

Appetizer

Salmon Rillette Canapés
Light and fresh with just a hint of fresh dill
on whole wheat baguette toast

Salad

Pea Tendril Salad
A tangle of fresh pea greens and seared scallops dressed
with a citrus vinaigrette and served
on a fresh, crisp, savory
masa de arepa (corn cake)

Main Course

Veal Chops in the French Style
Individual chops seared, then coated in herbed Dijon mustard and
seasoned bread crumbs

Asparagus with Mushroom Jus
Fresh, tender asparagus with baby Portobello mushrooms and a
mushroom and white wine reduction

Smashed Baby Reds
Baby red potatoes smashed with their skins on
and dressed with crème fraiche

Dessert

Stuffed Poire au Vin
Clove-studded Bosc pears poached in port wine and honey
and then stuffed with mascarpone cheese

Salmon Rillette Canapés

Poaching liquid
1/2 cup dry white wine
1 tablespoon champagne wine vinegar
1 shallot, minced
1 bay leaf
1 cup water
6 allspice berries
6 black peppercorns
6 green peppercorns
1 tablespoon lemon juice
1 tablespoon sugar
Salt to taste

Rillette
1/2 pound fresh salmon
1/2 pound smoked salmon
1/4 cup butter softened
2 tablespoons mayonnaise
1/4 cup heavy whipping cream
1 lemon juiced, use as needed
3 tablespoons lemon zest
1 bunch fresh dill, finely chopped, tops reserved
1 tablespoon fresh chives, minced
Salt and pepper to taste
2 whole wheat baguettes

Method:
To make the poaching liquid combine the poaching liquid ingredients (except salt and pepper) in an 8-inch sauté pan, bring to a boil and reduce by half. Season with salt and pepper and lower to a simmer.

To prepare the rillette, season the fresh salmon with salt and pepper and poach gently in the poaching liquid for 6 to 8 minutes or until cooked through. Remove from the poaching liquid to cool. Discard liquid. When cool, flake it into small pieces.

Puree the smoked salmon and cream until smooth in a food processor fitted with the metal processing blade. Remove to a mixing bowl and fold in the room temperature butter, then fold in the flaked salmon, followed by the mayonnaise, lemon zest, chopped dill and minced chives. Drip in lemon juice until you get to the desired consistency. Taste and adjust seasonings. Cover and refrigerate for at least two hours before assembling canapés.

Slice and lightly toast the baguettes. Spread each piece with some of the rillette and garnish with a sprig of the reserved dill. This can be fancied up with a few grains of salmon roe as garnish. Makes 48 canapés.

Pea Tendril Salad

Masa de Arepa
1 cup cornmeal
1/2 cup white flour
1/2 cup corn kernels, fresh or frozen
2 egg yolks
1/2 cup shredded parmesan cheese
1 1/2 cups hot water
2 teaspoons fresh thyme, minced
1 teaspoon fresh basil, minced
Salt and pepper to taste

Method:
Combine the cornmeal, flour and salt. Add water and beaten egg yolks and mix into a soft dough. Use plastic wrap to cover and let the dough stand for about 5 minutes. Knead for another 3 minutes or until smooth. If the dough isn't moist enough, wet your hands and continue kneading, repeating until the dough is soft. Mix in remaining ingredients and shape into small discs, about 4 inches in diameter and 1/4 inch thick. To cook, heat a cast-iron skillet or griddle over medium heat. Grease it lightly with oil and cook discs on both sides until a crust forms. This should take 5 to 10 minutes. Place on ungreased baking sheets and finish in a 350-degree, preheated oven for another 10 to 15 minutes. Makes 8 to 10 arepas.

Pea Tendril Salad
1/2 pound scallops
12 ounces pea tendrils
1/4 cup olive oil
1/8 cup fresh lemon juice
1 teaspoon celery seed
Salt and pepper to taste

Method:
Heat a large sauté pan over medium-high heat. Toss scallops in 1 tablespoon of the olive oil, celery seed and salt and pepper to taste. Sear scallops on both sides in the hot sauté pan and set aside. In a large mixing bowl, just before serving, drizzle olive oil and lemon juice over pea tendrils, season with salt and pepper and toss until lightly coated.

To assemble the salads, place an arepa in the center of a salad plate, top with pea tendrils and 3-5 scallops depending on the size. Makes six servings.

Veal Chops the French Way

1 1/2 pounds veal chops (6 individual chops)
2 tablespoons canola oil
8 ounces Dijon mustard
1 cup seasoned bread crumbs
2 tablespoons fresh oregano, minced
1 shallot, minced
2 tablespoons white wine
Salt and pepper to taste

Method:

Preheat oven to 325 degrees.

French or scrape the ends of the bones. Heat a large sauté pan over medium high heat to almost smoking. Coat chops with oil and season with salt and pepper. Sear on both sides and remove to a platter. Sear in batches so as to not crowd the pan. In a small mixing bowl combine the mustard and white wine and stir oregano and minced shallot. Coat each chop with the mustard mixture, shaking off the excess and leaving frenched bone clean. Coat with bread crumbs and place on roasting rack in a roasting pan. Slow roast covered to desired doneness. Makes 6 servings.

Asparagus with Mushroom Jus

1 1/2 pounds baby Portobello mushrooms
1 tablespoon canola oil
2 shallots, peeled, minced
1 clove garlic, minced
1 1/2 cups chicken stock
1 cup dry white wine
3 pounds fresh asparagus (24 to 36 spears) ends trimmed
2 tablespoons butter
2 tablespoons fresh chives, minced
12 sprigs fresh chervil (garnish)
Salt and pepper to taste

Method:

Heat the oil over medium heat in a large sauté pan. Add the shallot and garlic and cook until softened. Add the mushrooms, season with salt and pepper, and cook for 6 to 8 minutes. Add the stock and 3/4 cup of the wine. Bring to a boil and then reduce the heat and simmer for about 5 minutes. Cover, remove from heat and set aside to keep warm. Fill a large sauce pan with water, salt and bring to a boil over medium-high heat. Blanch the asparagus spears for 4 or 5 minutes or until just tender when pierced with a sharp knife. Cook the asparagus in batches to avoid over crowding the pan and over-cooking the asparagus. Drain them on a kitchen towel. Arrange asparagus on plates and, using a slotted spoon, distribute the mushrooms evenly. Top with the chives. Over high heat, reheat the mushroom jus to boiling, allow to reduce slightly to intensify the flavors, taste and adjust the seasoning. Remove from the heat and stir in the remaining quarter cup of wine and swirl in the butter. Makes 6 servings. Serve over the asparagus.

Smashed Baby Reds

2 pounds red potatoes, washed, quartered
4 ounces crème fraiche
2 ounces butter
Salt and white pepper to taste

Method:

In a large sauce pan, boil quartered red potatoes until fork tender. Drain thoroughly. Mash potatoes and mix in crème fraiche and butter, season to taste.

Stuffed Poire au Vin

2 pounds Bosc pears (6 pears)
2 cups honey
2 cups port wine
2 cups Marsala wine
2 cinnamon sticks
1/8 teaspoon mace
8 ounces mascarpone cheese, softened
30 whole cloves

Method:

Combine the honey, wine, cinnamon and mace in a medium-sized, straight-sided pan and heat until well combined.

Meanwhile peel the pears, leaving them whole and leaving the stems intact. Use a melon baller to remove the core from the blossom end of each pear. Stud each pear with 5 whole cloves. Place pears in wine mixture and add boiling water if needed to cover the pears. Cover and cook gently until the fruit is tender. This should take about 15 to 20 minutes. When done, remove the pears from the cooking liquid and let drain and cool. Return the poaching liquid to the heat and simmer uncovered until reduced to about 2 cups. Remove cinnamon sticks. When the pears are cool, stuff the cavities with softened mascarpone cheese, stand upright in individual deep serving dishes and pour reduced cooking liquid over and around the fruit.

This was one of the views Doug and Glenn had when they lived in Antigua.

About the chef ... Doug Janousek

This country is often referred to as a melting pot, a combination of cultures, races and ethnicities unlike any other in history. As such, defining American culture can be difficult sometimes because it depends on what part of the country you're talking about.

Popular culture is one thing, as depicted in television, movies and the proliferation of fast food and chain restaurants. And while these images are somewhat accurate, we all know there is much more to us as a people than action movies, situation comedies and drive-through hamburgers and french fries.

Take food, for instance. Some foods speak of a region like no other. Gumbo: Louisiana. Clam chowder: New England. Chicken fried steak: Texas. Citrus and seafood: Florida. Salmon, halibut, moose chili: Alaska.

Here you are, almost half way through this book, and you've been exposed to a variety of cooking styles, ingredients and kitchen traditions. With seven more cooking chapters to go, you can be sure the variety will continue.

Of course, our food traditions can be traced back to whatever part of the world our forbearers came from, which we then blend with local ingredients and methods we pick up from our neighbors and friends wherever we settle.

I've gathered recipes and cooking ideas from all the places I've lived (in chronological order): Nebraska, South Dakota, Florida, Antigua in the Caribbean, Massachusetts, Nevada, Texas, California, back to Florida, Alaska and finally back to Florida again.

We might use the recipes we learned from Mom and Grandma, be we use them with the local food that's available. If you are one of those cooks who can't or doesn't stray from the recipe, you could run into problems if you happen to be out of an ingredient and live someplace best described as remote. If the nearest grocery store is 30, 40 or 50 miles away, perhaps you'd be better off substituting something.

Granted, in this day of supermarkets you can get just about anything at anytime. With the way food is produced in this country, even "out-of-season" products can be obtained whenever you want.

But is this a good thing?

There's something to be said for buying locally grown goods whenever you can, which means you get what's fresh and in season, picked at its peak of flavor. If nothing else, it makes you appreciate it more if you can't get it all the time. The farmer's market is a great place to find local garden goodies (if you don't have your own) that are in-season, fresh and tasty.

www.home-cookin.net

49

June

June is my birth month, as well as the first month of summer. My menu is really very simple but packed with flavor and textures.

There is an Asian feel to the dinner with a little Southern touch thrown in. My husband and I love to go deep sea fishing and have often caught yellowfin tuna. I have served this meal on several occasions and, in fact, it is one that is often requested by friends and family.

The salad I chose is a recipe I had at a friend's house in Vero Beach several years ago. It is my husband's favorite salad, hence the name.

The dressing is a little sweet and a little sour. The nuts and rice noodles add a pleasing crunch and I think it makes a nice combination. I love the sweet cranberries with the scallions' pungency. It is very refreshing on a summer day.

Tuna is best cooked rare so that it doesn't dry out. I always try to buy more than I need for dinner so there will be enough for a fresh tuna salad the next day.

I pop the extra fish into the microwave on high in 20-second intervals until the meat is barely pink in the center. Make your tuna salad and refrigerate it for lunch the next day.

The vegetable casserole is the Southern touch I mentioned.

I like to cook this in a clear pie plate so I can see the layers as it cooks and all forms together. To serve, invert it onto a clean and decorative wooden chopping board such as a bamboo board. It really makes a nice presentation.

The finishing touch – CHOCOLATE of course! The recipe is very easy, just make sure you allow enough time for it to cool and set up.

I buy the pre-made pastry shells (pie shells); they save time and are very reliable. You can bake it as a pie with a meringue top – just be sure to bake the shell before adding the pudding. Or, cut the pastry into decorative shapes with cookie cutters and serve the pudding in martini glasses with the decorative pastry sticking up.

Garnish with some fresh berries.

– Chef Mary Sue Brannon

Salad

Stan's Favorite Salad

Main Course

Crustless Fresh Veggie Pie

Peppered Sesame Tuna Steaks

Dessert

Comfort Chocolate Pudding

Stan's Favorite Salad

5 ounces Romaine lettuce
5 ounces Iceberg lettuce
6 ounces Chinese rice noodles or croutons
2 ounces mixed nuts (roasted sunflower seeds, pecans, almonds)
2 ounces Romano cheese, shredded
1 ounce dried cranberries
2 ounces scallions, chopped

Method:

Wash and drain greens.
In a large salad bowl, toss the first six ingredients together.

Dressing

4 tablespoons dark brown sugar
6 tablespoons seasoned red wine vinegar
1/2 cup vegetable oil

Method:

Whisk all ingredients together.
Just before serving, coat greens with dressing and garnish with scallions.

Crustless Fresh Veggie Pie

1 clove garlic, peeled and sliced in half
2 large ripe tomatoes
2 small zucchini and/or yellow summer squash
1 large red or gold potato, peeled
4 ounces mushrooms, sliced
6 ounces asparagus, chopped
1/2 cup red onion, chopped
1 small shallot, chopped
1 1/2 cups shredded Gruyere cheese, divided
2 eggs, lightly beaten
1 teaspoon salt
1/4 teaspoon ground black pepper
2 teaspoons Italian seasoning
1/4 cup fresh bread crumbs

Method:

Heat the oven to 400 degrees.

Using a glass pie plate or casserole dish, rub the bottom and sides with the sliced garlic and coat with cooking spray.

Slice the tomato in half through the stem, then cut crosswise into slices. Cover the bottom of the pie plate with the sliced tomato pieces.

Cut the squash and potato into quarter pieces lengthwise and then cut crosswise into thin slices.

In a large bowl, combine the next nine ingredients and toss to mix well.

Pour over the tomato in the pie plate. Make sure it is even and tightly packed. Sprinkle the remaining cheese and bread crumbs on top.

Bake for 40 to 45 minutes or until the vegetables are tender and the cheese is golden brown. Invert on to a wooden board and garnish with fresh basil leaves.

If serving in the dish, top with chopped fresh tomatoes and a sprig of fresh basil.

Peppered Sesame Tuna Steaks

4 tuna steaks, cut one inch thick
1/2 cup reduced sodium Tamari soy sauce
2 tablespoons crushed black peppercorns
Salt to taste
2 tablespoons white sesame seeds
2 tablespoons black sesame seeds
2 tablespoons butter

Method:

Place the tuna steaks in a pie plate and coat each side with crushed peppercorns.

Add the Tamari soy sauce and marinate on counter top for 10 minutes.

While the tuna is marinating, heat an iron skillet on medium high until very hot, but not smoking.

Remove tuna steaks from marinade. Sprinkle lightly with salt (be careful because the soy sauce is salty as well).

Mix black and white sesame seeds together (you can use all white or all black if you want). Coat both sides of tuna with the sesame seed mix.

Place the tuna in the hot skillet and cook for 3 minutes on each side. Do not overcook the tuna. It should still be pink on the inside with just a white outline on the outside.

Comfort Chocolate Pudding

1 package of ready-made pie crust
4 ounces bittersweet chocolate, chopped
1 cup sugar
2 tablespoons strong brewed coffee
1/4 cup cornstarch
Pinch salt
3 cups milk (whole or skim)
3 egg yolks at room temperature, beaten
1 1/4 teaspoon pure vanilla extract
2 tablespoons butter
Fresh fruit for garnish

Method:

Roll out pie crust and cut various decorative shapes according to manufacturer's directions.

Combine the chocolate, sugar, coffee, cornstarch and salt in a saucepan and mix well. Add the milk. Bring to a gentle boil over medium heat, stirring occasionally. Once at a gentle boil, cook mixture for 3 minutes, stirring continually.

In a separate bowl, temper the eggs with some of the hot mixture by combining 1/2 cup of the hot mixture with the beaten egg yolks and mixing well. Slowly, add this mixture back into the saucepan and continue to cook for 2 minutes more.

Remove the pan from the heat and add the vanilla extract and butter.

Pour into a bowl and let cool slightly. Place plastic wrap on top of the pudding to prevent skin from forming.

Once cooled, place in decorative individual bowls and garnish with fruit and cut-out shapes from the pie crust.

About the chef ... Mary Sue Brannon

My husband, Stan, and I just celebrated our 25th wedding anniversary. In reflecting on that, I remember how much my cooking has improved.

I have always enjoyed being in the kitchen. When I was a little girl in Memphis, Tennessee, my grandmother would put me up on the counter to help her and to watch her cook. She was a very short woman and having me on the counter served two purposes: one, to be where she could see me and the other, to hand her things from the cabinets.

I felt involved and learned a lot from watching her. She would stand at her gas stove and make hot chocolate for her grandchildren. To this day whenever I smell the gas from a gas oven or burner I think of her.

We love to spend our free time on our boat fishing with our two small dogs, Chloe and Teika. They love to sun bathe in the cockpit while we are tossing lines. We have caught many species of fish including mahi-mahi (dolphin fish), yellowfin tuna, wahoo, yellowtail snapper, grouper, as well as the big game fish marlin and sailfish. I am always trying new recipes with the fresh fish we catch. I love to cook on the grill and being in Florida we get to do that all year long.

I am a graduate of Orlando Culinary Academy, Le Cordon Bleu Program. Though I got started professionally cooking late in life, I have cooked full meals since I was 16 years old.

I wanted to go to culinary school to hone my skills and to do something that I really love to do. I learned a lot through school and the mentoring I received from the chefs there is of immeasurable value.

Since graduating, my friend Marla Zell and I started a personal chef business. After learning many new experiences in our business, I have branched out on my own under the name of Chefs On The Way, LLC. Marla and I do keep in touch and know that we can count on each other in future endeavors.

Cooking aside, I love to eat as well and have a furious appetite. A very good friend is the same way and she once told me that her husband teased her that she had an appetite like a Marine. When I told my husband the story, he said, "Did you tell her that you have an appetite like a lumber-jack?"

I get a kick out of telling that story because it is so true. I hope you enjoy the menu I have selected for this book. For other ideas, questions, or new recipes for your kitchen please email me at chefsontheway@yahoo.com.

July

Florida in July is as hot as the firecrackers exploding to celebrate Independence Day. As a native Floridian, I have called both Central and South Florida home.

My happiest memories include trips to Flagler Beach for the Fourth of July. My maternal grandmother cleverly created a "Fourth of July Princess" costume for me made of red, white and blue crepe paper and entered me in the local parade.

July is an incredible month for picnics, barbecues and outdoor entertaining. Presenting a bountiful buffet, offering each guest a sampling of many different menu items, is my favorite way to entertain.

The menu I have designed is a tribute to different types of Florida produce and includes a signature recipe, Pineapple Cheese Casserole from my very special mom, Maureen Talton.

The menu begins with Fried Green Plantains, as prepared by my husband, who spent time living in both Cuba and Puerto Rico until joining the Air Force.

Watermelon Blast Off is a refreshing aperitif, taking advantage of the fruit at its sweetest (May through July).

Fire and Ice Salad screams for flavorful fresh tomatoes. Ugly Ripes, grown in Plant City, Florida, are an excellent choice for the salad. Heirloom tomatoes are also a wonderful choice.

These non-hybrid varieties cannot be called heirloom unless they have been in existence for 40-50 years. They are open pollinated and kept in their "true to form" state. They are available in many sizes and colors and are packed with flavor.

My absolute favorite Florida fruit is the key lime. Originating in South Asia, the fruit was brought by Arabs across North Africa to Spain and Portugal, whose explorers then transported the fruit to the West Indies, the Caribbean basin and, eventually to South Florida.

Double Trouble Key Lime Pie is one of my favorite ways to use this little powerhouse of flavor.

Enjoy this hot, summertime "Taste of Florida!"

– Chef Marla Zell

July Fourth Picnic Buffet

Watermelon Blast Off

Fried Green Plantains with Cilantro Garlic Sauce

Fried Garlic Picnic Chicken

Tarragon Potato Salad

Fire and Ice Salad

"Kitchen Sink" Pasta Salad

Mo's Pineapple Cheese Casserole

Sassy Grilled Bread

Double Trouble Key Lime Pie

Watermelon Blast Off

4 Key limes or 2 Persian limes
3 cups seedless watermelon pulp, pureed
1/4 cup fresh mint leaves, finely chopped
4 teaspoons Turbinado sugar
1 1/2 cups white rum
3 cups sparkling water or club soda
Crushed ice
Lime wheels and mint sprigs for garnish

Method:

Zest limes and mince zest finely.

Juice limes into serving pitcher.

Add watermelon puree, chopped mint leaves, sugar and minced lime zest. Using a muddler or mortar, mash ingredients well, making sure to dissolve sugar into mixture.

Add rum, sparkling water or club soda and stir.

Fill tall glasses with crushed ice and serve mixture over ice.

Garnish glasses with lime wheel and/or mint sprigs.

Sassy Grilled Bread

1 cup butter
1/3 cup Worcestershire sauce
1/3 cup fresh lemon juice
1 large loaf French or Italian bread, sliced on bias 1 inch thick, ends discarded

Method:

Combine butter, Worcestershire sauce and lemon juice in small saucepan and heat until butter melts. Whisk sauce ingredients together.

Preheat grill for low heat cooking.

Load bread slices onto a sheet of aluminum foil wide enough to enclose bread for warmth after grilling.

Arrange bread on preheated grill in as few rows as possible, allowing space sufficient for use of tongs to turn slices.

Moving quickly, brush the butter mixture on the exposed side of the slices, without worrying about fully covering each slice. Quickly turn the slices over and brush the exposed side with the butter mixture, now covering most of each surface.

Again, quickly turn each slice to the original side and reapply the butter mixture, taking care to fully cover each surface this time.

Every 90 seconds or so, turn slices to encourage browning and to touch up any bare spots with butter mixture.

Continue process until slices are golden brown and edges are crispy. Remove slices to aluminum foil and enclose bread to retain warmth until serving.

Mo's Pineapple Cheese Casserole

2 cans (20-ounce) chunk pineapple, drained
1 cup sugar mixed with 5 tablespoons flour
1 1/2 cups shredded sharp cheddar cheese
1 sleeve Ritz Crackers, crushed
1/2 cups butter, melted

Method:
Preheat oven to 350 degrees.
Grease a 12" x 8" baking pan.
Divide ingredient list in half and layer in order given.
Repeat for second layer.
Bake for 30 minutes.

Fried Green Plantains

4-5 large green plantains
Peanut oil for frying
Kosher salt
Bowl of salted water

Method:
Peel plantains with a sharp paring knife by removing ends and scoring the skin along the natural edges of the plantain, using the tip of the knife. Again using the tip of the knife, separate the green skin from the tan flesh of the plantain and peel as a banana, using the knife when necessary.

Slice the peeled plantains on a slight bias into 3/4-inch slices.

Quickly add slices to the bowl of salty water, ensuring all slices are fully submerged.

Pour enough peanut oil to reach 1/4 inch depth in 14-inch skillet and preheat oil to 325-345 degrees.

Remove 6-8 plantain slices from salt water and pat dry with paper towel.

Fry slices in oil, turning occasionally, until light golden colored.

Transfer to a paper towel and cool slightly.

Repeat this process until all slices are done.

When slices are cool enough to handle, place them, one slice at a time, between 2 sheets of heavy parchment paper or a brown market bag. Mash slice to 1/4 inch thickness using a meat mallet or other heavy flat object.

Return slices to heated oil and fry, turning occasionally, to a rich golden brown color and crunchy texture.

Remove slices from oil, drain on a paper towel and salt to taste. Serve with cilantro-garlic sauce.

Cilantro-Garlic Sauce

8 garlic cloves
1 cup cilantro leaves, packed
2 tablespoons shallots, finely chopped
1 tablespoon fresh lime juice
1 cup olive oil
1 teaspoon Kosher salt
3/4 teaspoon hot pepper sauce

Method:

In a food processor or blender, combine all ingredients and process until mixture is blended. Serve alongside fried plantains.

Fire and Ice Salad

6 assorted heirloom tomatoes, cored and cut into wedges
1 sweet onion, sliced
1 red, yellow, or orange pepper, sliced into strips
1 seedless cucumber, peeled and sliced
1/3 cup Balsamic vinegar
1/4 cup sugar or equivalent artificial sweetener
1 tablespoon Dijon mustard
2 garlic cloves, minced
1/2 teaspoon Kosher salt
1/2 teaspoon seasoned pepper or freshly ground black pepper
1/2 cup olive oil
1/3 cup fresh basil

Method:

Combine vegetables in a large serving bowl.

Process vinegar, sugar, mustard, garlic, salt and pepper in a blender or food processor until smooth.

With processor or blender running on slow speed, add olive oil slowly until mixture is smooth.

Just before serving, stack basil leaves together and roll into a "cigar." With a sharp knife, slice the basil thinly into strips.

Add dressing to vegetables, toss and toss again with fresh basil.

Fried Garlic Picnic Chicken

3 cups buttermilk
4 tablespoons fresh lemon juice
4 garlic cloves, smashed
1 teaspoon Kosher salt
1/2 teaspoon celery salt
1/2 teaspoon seasoned black pepper
8 large skinless bone-in chicken breasts
2 cups seasoned flour (available pre-seasoned on the baking aisle in the supermarket)
Peanut oil for frying

Method:

Combine the first 6 ingredients and pour into a large, shallow, marinating pan with tight cover.

Add chicken, cover the pan and flip it over several times to saturate the chicken. Refrigerate at least 4 hours or overnight for best flavor.

Remove chicken from liquid and dredge in seasoned flour.

Heat 1 inch of oil in cast-iron skillet or electric skillet to 325 degrees.

Fry chicken 30-35 minutes, turning once halfway through.

Remove and drain well on cooling rack placed over paper towel-covered grocery bag.

Tarragon Potato Salad

3 pounds red skinned new potatoes
4 tablespoons green onion, minced
Tarragon Dressing (recipe follows)
Italian parsley, finely chopped
Paprika

Method:

Place unpeeled potatoes into saucepan, cover with water and bring to a boil. Reduce heat and simmer potatoes 15 minutes or until tender when pierced.

Prepare Tarragon Dressing.

Drain potatoes and peel when cooled. Slice into 1/4 inch slices.

Toss potatoes in serving bowl with minced green onion and enough dressing to evenly moisten the salad. Garnish with chopped fresh Italian parsley and sprinkle with paprika. Cover and chill if not serving immediately.

Tarragon Dressing

1 hard boiled egg
2 tablespoons fresh tarragon leaves or 2 teaspoons dried
1 1/2 tablespoons fresh Italian parsley or 1 1/2 teaspoons dried

1 1/2 teaspoons dry mustard powder
1 teaspoon Kosher salt
1 teaspoon white pepper
2 tablespoons fresh lemon juice
4 garlic cloves, chopped
3 green onions, minced
1/3 cup tarragon vinegar
1 1/2 cups sunflower or vegetable oil

Method:

Combine all ingredients, except the vinegar and the oil, in a blender or food processor. Process for 30 seconds or to the consistency of a smooth puree.

Add vinegar to the puree and process until blended.

With motor running, slowly add oil in a steady stream until the dressing appears pale green and smooth. Store refrigerated in covered container.

"Kitchen Sink" Pasta Salad

16-ounce package gemelli, farfalle (bowtie) or wagon wheel pasta
1/4 cup olive oil
Kosher salt and fresh ground pepper to taste
2 jars (11- to 12-ounce) marinated artichoke hearts, drained and quartered
1/2 cup fire roasted red peppers, cut in strips
1 jar (3-ounce) capers, drained
1/2 cup Kalamata olives, pitted and halved
12 oil-packed sun dried tomatoes, drained and cut into strips
1/2 cup freshly grated Parmesan cheese
1/3 cup fresh Italian parsley, chopped
5 cloves garlic, minced
3/4 cup olive oil
1/4 cup white balsamic vinegar
1/4 cup fresh lemon juice
1 hard boiled egg yolk
1 tablespoon fresh chopped basil or 1 teaspoon dried
1 teaspoon dry mustard powder
1/4 teaspoon Kosher salt
1/8 teaspoon white pepper
1/4 teaspoon mild hot sauce
1/2 cup pine nuts, toasted (on stove top over medium heat in small dry skillet, stirring frequently and watching like a hawk!)

Method:

Cook pasta according to package directions, drain and place in large serving bowl.

Toss gently with 1/4 cup olive oil, salt and pepper to taste.

Add artichoke hearts, roasted peppers, olives, capers, sun dried tomatoes, Parmesan cheese and parsley. Combine gently and set aside while preparing dressing.

In the bowl of a food processor or heavy duty blender, add garlic, followed by all the remaining ingredients except for the pine nuts. Process until smooth.

Pour dressing over pasta mixture and combine gently. Cover and marinate in refrigerator one hour or more.

Sprinkle toasted pine nuts over salad just before serving.

Double Trouble Key Lime Pie

For the crust:
6 tablespoons butter, melted
1 1/2 cups finely crushed cream-filled vanilla sandwich cookies (around 15-16)
1 cup sweetened flaked coconut

Method:
Preheat oven to 350 degrees.

Place coconut on a baking sheet and bake 7-10 minutes, stirring frequently, until lightly browned.

Combine toasted coconut and cookies with butter and press firmly into a 9-inch pie pan.

Cover and chill 30 minutes prior to filling.

For the filling, first layer:
1 can (14-ounce) sweetened condensed milk
1/2 cup fresh Key lime juice
3 large egg yolks

Method:
Beat egg yolks lightly, then stir in condensed milk. Add lime juice and beat until smooth.

Pour mixture into pie crust.

Bake 25 minutes, or until filling is set.

Cool to room temperature.

For the filling, second layer:
8 ounces cream cheese, room temperature
1/2 cup sweetened condensed milk
1/4 cup fresh Key lime juice
2 tablespoons sugar
1 teaspoon dark rum (or 1 teaspoon vanilla extract, if preferred)

Method:
With electric mixer, beat cream cheese, milk, lime juice, sugar and rum or vanilla extract in a large mixing bowl. Pour over the cooled baked layer and smooth the top.

Cover and chill until firm, a minimum of 5 hours.

Top with whipped cream, if desired.

About the chef ... Marla Zell

A native Floridian, Marla Zell, first enjoyed cooking in her Swedish grandmother's kitchen.

Following graduation from Georgia Tech, she pursued a lifelong dream to be a flight attendant. What was to have been a brief career progressed into 31 years flying for two major airlines.

Traveling within the United States, as well as internationally, afforded her the opportunity to become acquainted with a variety of foods.

As her passion for cooking grew, so did the desire to receive professional training which resulted in enrollment at Orlando Culinary Academy, where she graduated summa cum laude and received a degree in culinary arts.

After graduation, she and a fellow culinary classmate started their own personal chef business.

One of her favorite endeavors is creating wedding and special occasion cakes.

Chef Zell has attended the Wilton School for Cake Decorating Master Course.

Currently, Chef Zell is working on the creation of her own company, A Food Affaire. Services and products will be available at afoodaffaire.com, currently under construction.

She says participating in this cookbook has been an honor and very enjoyable.

August

For the month of August I chose a Vietnamese inspired menu. I was fortunate enough to make a two-week culinary tour of Vietnam, from the south to the north.

The food was always fresh, sometimes spicy and different everywhere we went. The open air markets with all of the fresh (and sometimes still alive) products were amazing.

August is a hot month and these are all hot weather foods. Some are spicy, which is common in hot regions of the world. You eat, sweat and then cool off with something cold like fruit and beverages.

These recipes are my interpretation of some of the dishes we experienced.

The seared tofu salad was a dish prepared for us at the KOTO school for disadvantaged street kids. The warmth and hospitality with which we were received was overwhelming.

Hue, an instructor in training, walked us through this delicious salad, cold and crisp with a refreshing dressing accompanied by seared tofu triangles. This was a new sensation for us and we loved it.

Miss Tuyet's spring rolls were some of the best we tasted and we tasted some spring rolls. A nice thick white fish will be just delicious in the light fresh rolls and of course don't forget the fish sauce!

Water Morning Glory is another food we tried everywhere we went. It resembles broccoli rabe, which can be used as a substitute. It is delicious hot or cold.

Hue cakes are a specialty of Hue, a beautiful town with the friendliest people we met. We had the pleasure of having a cooking class and dinner in an authentic garden house. We felt like kings. The open walled houses, all connected by pathways and surrounded by beautiful foliage and water, was the perfect setting.

We had the steamed Hue cakes wrapped in banana leaf. When the cakes are done you open the banana leaves and scoop out the savory warm surprise inside.

Grilled beef in lot leaves is reminiscent of tofu stuffed grape leaves, but grilled and served on a skewer. The grill flavor is a perfect accompaniment to the beef and Asian flavors in the leaf.

When you've had your fill of the various dishes and some of the pepper is working, you can cool off with a cool fruit salad, a perfect end to an amazing meal.

– Chef Dale Pyle

Asian Buffet

Black Sea Bass Spring Roll
A delicious alternative to the average spring roll, inspired by Miss Tuyet,
one of Tony Bourdain's favorite chefs

Hue Cake
Heaven in a banana leaf

Seared Tofu Salad
Lightly browned tofu with marinated tomatoes, cucumbers and greens

Water Morning Glory Salad
A Vietnamese delicacy

Grilled Beef in Lot Leaves
Grilled stuffed lot leaves with a savory filling – think stuffed grape
leaves with an Asian twist

Fruit Salad with Coconut and Honey

Seared Tofu Salad

1 pound tofu
6 tablespoons grated fresh ginger
10 tablespoons soy sauce
24 scallions, sliced thin on the bias
8 tablespoons vegetable oil
1 tablespoon sesame oil
2 heads Bibb or young lettuce torn into bite size pieces
2 medium tomatoes, sliced
1 hothouse cucumber
6 tablespoons Asian sweet chili sauce
5 ounces crushed peanuts
2 tablespoons sesame seeds toasted

Method:

Cut tofu into bite-sized triangles.

Prepare tofu marinade using the ginger, soy, sesame oil and half the onions. Gently mix marinade and tofu and set aside for 30 minutes.

Heat oil in frying pan and brown tofu evenly.

Arrange tofu around the edge of serving plates.

In a bowl, combine chili sauce, lettuce, tomato and cucumber. Toss gently.

Arrange lettuce in the middle of the plate and arrange tomatoes and cucumbers around lettuce.

Garnish with onions and sesame seeds. Sprinkle with chopped peanuts.

Four servings.

Water Morning Glory Salad

1 pound water morning glory (broccoli rabe can be substituted)
1/4 cup fresh lime juice
2 teaspoons sea salt
3 tablespoons yellow sesame seeds
3 ounces peanuts
1 teaspoon fresh marjoram, cleaned and picked
1 teaspoon chili peppers sliced thin

Method:

Blanch morning glory in salted water until just tender. Remove to ice bath, cool, then drain well.

Roast sesame and peanuts, then chop.

Mix morning glory, lime juice and a little salt.

Place salad on plate, garnish with peanuts and sesame seeds. Sprinkle marjoram and chilies around salad and a little on top. Four servings.

Grilled Beef in Lot Leaves

8 ounces ground beef
4 ounces ground pork
1 teaspoon chopped garlic
1 teaspoon chopped shallots
2 teaspoons chopped lemon grass
1 teaspoon oyster sauce
1 teaspoon soy sauce
2 teaspoons oil
Lot leaves or mustard leaves
Dipping sauce (recipe follows)

Method:

Combine beef, pork, lemongrass, garlic and shallot with seasonings and oyster sauce.

Spread leaves out on board, place a little filling on the edge, roll once, fold in sides and roll into a cylinder.

Skewer 3 or 4 rolls together and cook on grill until firm.

Serve with dipping sauce.

Dipping sauce

1 tablespoon Asian fish sauce
2 tablespoons sugar
1 tablespoon pineapple juice
Chopped garlic
Sliced chilies

Hue Cake

1 pound rice flour
1 pound shrimp
1/2 pound ground pork
1/2 gallon water
10 flowering chives or violet onion

Banana leaves
Asian fish sauce
Oil
Sugar
Salt and pepper

Method:

Cook shrimp in water, peel and chop fine. Reserve cooking water.

Slice onion thin. Add pork, shrimp and onion to sauté pan over medium heat.

Season with sugar, a teaspoon of fish sauce and pepper.

Cook until fairly dry. Set aside.

Stir rice flour into 2 1/2 cups boiling water that you used for the shrimp to make a smooth paste. Gradually add about another quart of the shrimp water, stirring steadily and add 2 tablespoons of oil. Stir until it becomes thick; do not overcook or mixture could curdle.

To assemble, take a spoonful of the flour mixture and form a small rectangle in the middle of a banana leaf. Top with a spoonful of shrimp and pork mixture.

Fold leaf and roll gently into a small packet.

Steam for about 7 minutes.

To serve, open leaves to expose cake and add a little fish sauce if desired.

Sea Bass Spring Roll

1 pound black sea bass
1 ounce fresh cilantro
4 or 5 scallions sliced
1/2 pound Napa cabbage shredded
2 ounces carrot shredded
5 or 6 woodear mushrooms sliced (re-hydrate in warm water if dry)
1 ounce rice vermicelli soaked in water
1 egg
20 sheets rice paper or 20 spring roll wrappers
1 ounce bird pepper minced
1/2 ounce Asian fish sauce
1 ounce sugar
1 ounce garlic minced
1/2 ounce rice vinegar
Vegetable oil for cooking

Method:

Steam or fry fish, flake apart and set aside.

Place cabbage, carrots, dill, mushrooms, vermicelli, sugar and cilantro in a bowl and mix in egg. Gently fold in fish.

Take a rice paper sheet and place a small amount of filling slightly off center. Fold the paper up to cover and tuck in tight. Fold in sides and then spread a little egg to seal edges. Roll tightly without ripping it and deep fry.

For dipping sauce:

Place garlic and chopped or sliced chili pepper in small dish and mix with vinegar, fish sauce and a little shredded carrot for garnish.

Fruit Salad

1 mango
1 papaya
1 pineapple
1 small seedless watermelon
Berries for garnish
Honey
Toasted coconut
Mint leaves

Method:

Slice fruit and fan attractively on platter. Drizzle honey, sprinkle with coconut and garnish with berries and mint leaves.

About the chef ... Dale Pyle

I have more than 35 years of experience in the hospitality industry. A native Central Floridian from Melbourne, I have a wife and two children and am the proud owner of a personal chef company, "At Your Service PCS" in Altamonte

Springs, Florida.

Prior to joining the Orlando Culinary Academy as a chef instructor I served as executive chef at the Embassy Suites Hotel, the Heathrow Country Club and Waterman Village in Mount Dora, Florida.

My qualifications include:
B.S. Culinary Arts, Minor Management, Breyer State University 2004
Certified Executive Chef
Certified Hospitality Educator
Member American Culinary Federation
Member American Personal Chef Association
Member Les Amis d'Escoffier Society
Honorary Member Eta Sigma Delta
– International Hospitality and Tourism Management Society.

You can reach me at 407-260-0619.

September

While the weather in Florida doesn't make a drastic change from season to season, unless you count hurricane season, the kinds of activities here definitely mark the turning of the calendar.

September marks the end of summer with a frenzy of final barbecues and end-of-season picnics. School has just started and while hot days still lie ahead, we all know autumn is coming.

The tourists who flock to Florida for the beach experience as well as the theme-parks start to thin a little, so locals can reclaim a bit of their territory.

The extreme heat and humidity of the summer is just starting to wane, or at least we imagine it is, as we head for the grill.

With a frosty adult beverage in hand, it does seem a little cooler.

For a season-ending meal, nothing can beat something simple, starting with frosty strawberry soup, skewered shrimp and scallops, a refreshing tomato and mozzarella salad, moving on to grill-braised pork roast, a rice salad with sun-dried tomatoes and fresh fruit for a change of pace and finishing with home-made ice cream topped with fresh fruit and a cabernet syrup.

– Chef Doug Janousek

Soup

Strawberry Soup
Fresh berries and yogurt highlight this chilled sweet start
to one last party under the sun

Appetizer

Skewered Shrimp & Scallops
Ceviche-style seafood with a hint of cilantro, lemon and lime
and a dash of heat

Salad

Tomatoes & Mozzarella
Tomatoes, fresh Mozzarella and cool pesto

Main Course

Grill Braised Pork Roast
Fork tender and flavored with smoky onion

Rice Salad
Tender rice and fresh fruit for something a little different

Dessert

Fresh-Made Ice Cream
Creamy homemade ice cream, topped with fresh fruit
and Cabernet syrup

Strawberry Soup

1 quart strawberries, rinsed, dried, hulled and sliced
2 tablespoons coconut rum
1 tablespoon lemon juice
1/3 cup honey
2 cups plain yogurt
1 teaspoon vanilla extract

Method:

Place the strawberries, rum and lemon juice in a blender or food processor and blend until smooth. Force the mixture through a sieve to strain out the seeds. Return the fruit puree to the processor and blend with honey and yogurt until mixed. Chill before serving; serve in chilled bowls.

Skewered Shrimp & Scallops

12 large shrimp, peeled and deveined
12 large scallops, muscle tab removed
Grape tomatoes
1 large sweet onion, cut into large chunks
Juice of 6 fresh lemons
Juice of 6 fresh limes
Juice of 3 oranges
1 cup tomato juice
1 cup dry white wine
1 hot pepper, diced
1 bunch cilantro, stems removed
Salt and pepper to taste
Bamboo skewers

Method:

Prepare at least 4 hours before serving.

Skewer shrimp, scallops, tomatoes and pieces of onion, alternating seafood and vegetables.

Place in a shallow dish and cover with remaining ingredients, adding additional lemon and lime juice if liquid does not cover skewered seafood.

Chill for four hours.

Serve with crisp fried tortillas or as is, arranged on a platter.

Tomatoes & Mozzarella

4 Roma tomatoes, each sliced into 4-5 rounds
16 ounces fresh mozzarella, sliced into rounds
2 cups fresh basil leaves
1/4 cup pine nuts
3 cloves garlic
1/3 cup olive oil
1/2 cup grated Parmesan cheese
Salt and pepper to taste

Method:

Arrange tomato and cheese slices on salad plates.

In a food processor combine remaining ingredients, except the cheese and process in short bursts until smooth. Transfer to a bowl and stir in the cheese. Drizzle over tomato and cheese slices and serve.

Grill Braised Pork Roast

3-4 pound pork roast (Boston Butt)
3 large onions, peeled, cut in half
4 cloves garlic, peeled
2-3 bottles quality beer
Salt and pepper to taste

Method:

Preheat your grill and set for high heat.

Place onions and garlic in the bottom of a large cast-iron Dutch oven. Season roast and sear on all sides on the grill. Reduce heat on grill for low, slow cooking. Place roast in Dutch oven on top of onions and add first of the beer. Liquid should be at least three-quarters of the way up on the roast.

Cover and place on grill. Let it braise until you can smell the onions start to char, indicating that the liquid has mostly cooked away.

Add another beer, returning the liquid to original level. Cover and allow to continue cooking.

When you can smell the onions again, check roast for doneness (it should be fork tender). If it isn't quite done, add more beer, cover and let simmer. When it is ready, remove from grill, let rest for 10-15 minutes and serve.

Rice Salad

4 cups cooked rice (white or brown)
3 cups fresh spinach, trimmed, rough chopped
2 large avocados, peeled, pitted and diced
6 boiled eggs, peeled, diced
1 cup fresh chives, chopped
1/8 cup orange zest
1/2 cup sun dried tomatoes, julienne
1/2 cup mango, small dice
2 sweet oranges, peeled, sectioned (supremed)
1/4 cup pecans, chopped
1 cup goat cheese, crumbled
4 tablespoons olive oil
3 tablespoons red wine vinegar
Salt and pepper to taste

Method:

In a large bowl, toss together ingredients and let stand for about an hour. Taste and adjust seasoning.

Fresh-Made Ice Cream

3 cups sugar
6 tablespoons flour
4 cups milk, scalded
6 large eggs, beaten
5 cups heavy cream
5 tablespoons vanilla

Method:

Combine sugar and flour in a saucepan. Slowly stir in hot milk. Cook over low heat for about 10 minutes, stirring constantly until the mixture has thickened. Mix a small amount of the hot mixture into the beaten eggs. Add tempered eggs to hot mixture and cook for one more minute. Chill in refrigerator for 20 minutes. Add the cream and vanilla; pour into ice cream maker and freeze according to directions.

Cabernet Syrup

1 bottle Cabernet Sauvignon
1 cup honey
1 teaspoon vanilla

Method:

Combine ingredients in a saucepan and reduce by three-quarters. Cool slightly. Serve warm over ice cream. Top with sliced fresh fruit of your choice.

Wild horses race for the corral on a roundup near Hole in the Wall, Nevada, in August 1999 after a summer of wild fires destroyed much of their feed. Doug took this from a rock outcrop well above the thundering hooves.

About the chef ... Doug Janousek

Change happens to us whether we are ready for it or not.

The weather shifts, seemingly from one minute to the next and the only thing we can do is go with it – add a layer of clothes, take off the heavy coat, trade in the ankle socks for wool ones.

Being able to adapt is the single most important thing to succeeding.

Take being in the kitchen for example. You can plan everything out to the minute: all of your ingredients are lined up on the counter in the order you're going to use them. The sink is set up with hot soapy water, you have all your mixing bowls, utensils and pots and pans ready to go. And then something happens ... the milk is sour; you got involved in the soaps and time slipped away from you and you didn't get the roast on to braise; you go to start cooking and notice one of the younguns swiped your raisins for that special dessert and you don't have time to drive to town to get more . . . .

So, what do you do? Put everything away and set out a jar of peanut butter, a loaf of bread and tell the family to chow down? Order pizza? Head into town for Chinese takeout?

Well, those are all possibilities, but you could just adapt a little and make do with what you have.

When I originally wrote this, it was for my monthly food column in the Fairbanks News-Miner (yes, Fairbanks, Alaska).

I was addressing the changes in my life as I finished up the classroom portion of culinary school and was about to embark on my externship which would be the finishing touches on the Le Cordon Bleu program at the Orlando Culinary Academy.

Not that change has ever been a stranger to me. For those who have been following along, I moved around a lot as a journalist, not seeking the "big story" so much as seeking the perfect job. Though I had some great times along the way … hurricanes, desert fires, wild horse roundups, minus-40 in Alaska, Nor'easters in Massachusetts, a spewing volcano in the Caribbean, it turns out that for me finding the perfect job meant changing careers, not just locales.

In the original column, I waxed on about the change in my routine from school to the "real world," such as it is. I was looking forward to the 12 weeks of externship at the restaurant where I would work as a prep cook, as well as to the work I would be doing with a personal chef to show me the ropes a bit for what would become my next big adventure.

While I had a plan for those 12 weeks, I still kind of felt like someone swiped my raisins while I spent the best part of the day watching the soaps. Now what would I do? It is almost time for dinner and I haven't even started …

Without the structure of school it was like I was back in elementary school on the first day of summer vacation – No more pencils, no more books, no more chefs' dirty looks … my free time had been at a premium while I was in school, so with whole days off and no classroom structure, I was at a bit of a loss – do I sleep in or start on my project? Do I go out and enjoy the cooling weather or should I clean the apartment?

In other words, it was time for some mental mise en place so I could figure out what needs to be done and hopefully leave a little time to enjoy my new-found freedom.

While I looked forward to the changes to come, I continued to (and still do) keep an eye on what I've done and where I've been, because those experiences have made me who I am. Perhaps I could have made a different choice here and there, but I'd like to think I'm pretty clear-eyed about it with no regrets, because again, where I'm at is pretty good.

Whatever I've been confronted with along the way was well worth it.

My experience and the confidence I gathered along the way is reflected in my cooking, I think.

My knives feel comfortable in my hand and while ever watchful, I don't worry so much about leaving fingertips on the cutting board. I'm as comfortable surrounded by stainless steel tables, stack ovens and gas ranges with 10 burners as I am in front of this computer screen writing about it and as I am in anyone's home kitchen when I'm preparing their meals.

Culinary school was a great adventure and far more work and fun than I ever imagined. Starting my own business and combining personal chefing with freelance writing/editing/publishing is also a great adventure and far more work and fun than I ever imagined.

Having the opportunity to indulge my passions for cooking and writing is the most fun I've had personally and professionally.

I encourage everyone to indulge their passions, because life is far too short to do otherwise.

www.home-cookin.net

October

October is the very heart of the harvest season. Brilliant sunny days and lengthening cool nights inspire a sense of bounty and well-being, making it a perfect time for friends to come together over a festive meal.

Attempt this meal only when you are assured of the company of at least seven friends with healthy appetites.

A choucroute garnie is not for the timid or wary or the ubiquitous watchers-of-weight. This is a meal for people who like to eat and who prefer to wash down their hearty fare with quantities of chilled lager or dry white wine.

It is as much fun to make a choucroute garnie as it is to eat it. The dish is built on a foundation of mellow, tender, wine-soaked sauerkraut, which is then blessed with the rich earthy flavors of smoked meats and every kind of sausage you can lay your hands on. In France, a hot, spicy Lorraine sausage is one of the highlights of the feast.

Plan to begin cooking early – this dish takes eight or nine hours in a long, slow oven to come completely together. By the time you are ready to serve, your kitchen will be perfumed with the mouthwatering aromas of the harvest season.

– Chef Anne Mooney

Appetizer
Pate' of Forest Mushrooms on Melba Toasts
Small bites with an aroma redolent of earth and woods,
topped with a dollop of crème fraiche

Salad

Harvest Pears
Fall pears on a bed of field greens dressed with a spiced Balsamic
vinaigrette

Main Course

Choucroute Garnie
Aromatic sausages and smoked meats served on a bed of sauerkraut
seasoned with wine, onions, apples and juniper berries

Boiled Russet Potatoes
Fluffy, floury white potatoes, unadorned

Dessert

Tarte Tatin
Upside-down apple pie with a caramelized crust

Pate' of Forest Mushrooms on Melba Toasts

3/4 ounce dried wild mushrooms
1/4 cup butter
3/4 pound fresh brown mushrooms, sliced
1 garlic clove, minced
2 tablespoons brandy
1/4 cup whipping cream
1 teaspoon fresh thyme leaves
1/2 teaspoon juniper berries, ground
32 mini melba toasts
Crème fraiche and Italian flat leaf parsley for garnish

Method:

Soak dried mushrooms in bowl of hot (not boiling) water for one to two hours, or until soft. Drain, reserving 3 tablespoons of soaking liquid and discard any mushroom pieces that are still tough and woody.

Melt butter in large sauté pan over medium heat. Add fresh mushrooms and sauté for 5 minutes. Add garlic, cook about one minute, then add soaked dried mushrooms and their soaking liquid and sauté for an additional 5 to 8 minutes. Pour in brandy and cook until evaporated, about 2 minutes. Remove from heat and cool for about 10 minutes.

Transfer mushroom mixture to bowl of a food processor. Add whipping cream, thyme leaves, juniper berries and 1/2 teaspoon each of salt and pepper. Process mixture until very finely chopped.

Transfer pate' to bowl and refrigerate covered at least 3 hours, until fully chilled. Put a heaping teaspoon of pate' on each toast. Top with a dollop of crème fraiche and a parsley leaf.

Eight servings.

Salad of Harvest Pears

Baby lettuce or field greens
2 ripe Comice or Bosc pears, peeled and sliced
High-quality blue cheese, crumbled

For the dressing:
1/4 cup olive oil
1 tablespoon soy sauce
2 teaspoons rice vinegar
1 teaspoon Balsamic vinegar
1 teaspoon mirin or honey

Method:

Arrange greens on chilled salad plates. Arrange pears attractively on top of greens and crumble a little blue cheese over pears. Add dressing just before serving.

Eight servings.

Choucroute Garnie
Adapted from Robert Carrier, Great Dishes of the World (1963, Random House)

1 pound thinly sliced bacon
2 large yellow onions, sliced
2 tart apples, cored and sliced
4 large garlic cloves, coarsely chopped
4 pounds good quality sauerkraut, well rinsed
8 juniper berries, crushed
One bottle good quality Riesling or other dry white wine
2 cups chicken broth
1 boned pork loin
1 large garlic sausage
8 to 16 varied sausages (e.g., bratwurst, knockwurst, weisswurst, Toulouse)
8 slices of cooked ham
8 boiled russet potatoes

Method:
Preheat oven to 300 degrees.

Rinse sauerkraut well under cold running water and drain.

Line a deep, earthenware casserole with the bacon slices. Add half the onions, apples and chopped garlic. Top with a thick layer of rinsed and drained sauerkraut. Grind plenty of black pepper over it and sprinkle with juniper berries. Add remaining onions, apples and garlic, top with remaining sauerkraut and add just enough white wine to cover. Cover the casserole and bake at 300 degrees for at least 6 hours – the longer it cooks, the better. If sauerkraut begins to dry out, add chicken broth to moisten.

Add pork loin about 2 1/2 hours before serving. Two hours before serving, add the garlic sausage and a selection of the small sausages.

To serve, heap the choucroute in the midst of a large platter and arrange sausages and sliced meats around it. Serve with boiled potatoes and, if desired, slices of ham. A selection of 4 or 5 different mustards rounds out your presentation.

Eight hearty servings.

Tarte Tatin

1 stick (8 tablespoons) butter, cut into small pieces
1 teaspoon lemon juice
1 teaspoon ground cinnamon
6 tablespoons brown sugar
9 crisp tart apples – Jonagolds or Winesaps – peeled, cored and quartered
Pastry for a 9-inch pie (prepared pastry from the supermarket refrigerator case is fine for this)

Method:

Preheat oven to 350 degrees. Scatter 4 tablespoons butter and 3 tablespoons brown sugar evenly over the bottom of a 9-inch glass or ceramic pie plate. Roll out the pastry and stretch it over the butter and sugar, allowing it to drape evenly over the sides of the pie plate.

Tightly pack apple quarters, curved side down, in a spiral, covering the bottom surface of the pastry. Sprinkle apples with cinnamon, lemon juice and remaining 3 tablespoons brown sugar. Roll edges of pastry in toward the center, overlapping the outer edges of the apples.

Bake for about an hour, until apples caramelize to a golden brown and sugar and butter bubble. If pastry begins to brown too much, cover lightly with a sheet of aluminum foil.

When tart is done, remove from oven and loosen the pastry by gently running a small knife around the edge. Place a platter large enough to hold the tart on top of the pie plate. Carefully and quickly invert the tart so that the platter is on the bottom holding the tart upside down. Carefully remove the pie plate. Serve warm.

This tart is particularly good garnished with whipped crème fraiche into which you have stirred a tablespoon of apple brandy.

About the chef ... Anne Sears Mooney

I have been cooking or writing, or engaged in some combination of the two, for most of my adult professional life. Most recently, I was part of the marketing team at Whole Foods Market in the Mid-Atlantic region. Now I work as a personal

chef and freelance food writer in Central Florida.

My mother was an accomplished and adventurous cook at a time when that was less common than it is now. She and my father traveled all over the United States and Europe, exploring local customs and cuisines. Food played a central role in the romance they shared throughout their married life.

So it was at an early age that food came to represent community, festivity, adventure and romance to me and to my younger sister. As my sister and I grew up and moved away from home – both of us to New York – we continued to share in the joy of cooking and of writing about the

things we cooked and ate. In time, we learned to collaborate, in cooking lavish meals and in creating magazine articles and once, even a small book, to celebrate our shared passion for food.

Now, she and my parents are gone. This small effort is dedicated to them and to the adventure of food that we shared. This meal was a favorite in our household, one that evokes fond memories of festive meals, not a few glasses of good, dry Riesling, as well as the warmth and fellowship of friends and family around the table.

I hope you enjoy it!

I can be reached at (407) 671-2964 or via e-mail to annemooney@earthlink. net. Check out my Web site at www.chefannemooney.com.

November

November.

Just say the word. Heck, just think it and images of Thanksgiving pop into your head. Nearly everyone has a favorite Thanksgiving story and almost all of them revolve around food – a special meal, a favorite dish, sometimes a fabulous mistake that turned into a family joke.

Few days are anticipated as much as Thanksgiving Day. Well, Christmas and your birthday come to mind, but the beauty of Thanksgiving is that it is all about the food. Well, okay, football and parades, but when it comes down to it, it is the food.

And woe to anyone who messes with the menu. We all know what it is and how it goes: roast turkey, stuffing, green bean casserole, sweet potatoes, cranberries, mashed potatoes and pumpkin pie. Sure, you can come up with a variety of different side dishes, but the basics better be there.

An adventurous chef might attempt to come up with a different twist on these basics, but he or she has to remember the competition isn't another chef down the street, but years of memory and tradition of how Mom and Grandma made it. Those are hard acts to follow.

So, what about the other 29-odd days of the month?

Folks have to eat on those days too, which makes those other nights a great place to tinker with the tastes of the season without violating tradition.

– Chef Doug Janousek

Appetizer

Sweet Potato Pancakes
Crispy fried pancakes served with spiced crème fraiche

Salad

Honey, Pears & Cranberries
A sweet, tart variation of a traditional favorite, served on buttery
Boston Bibb lettuce

Soup

Roasted Pumpkin Soup
Creamy, spicy and just a touch of sweet and some heat,
served in the shell

Main Course

Turkey with Curried Currant Sauce
Roasted turkey breast with a touch of the Caribbean

Greens & Brown Rice
Fresh, wilted greens, earthy brown rice

Dessert

Ricotta Torte with Mixed Berries
Light and creamy, yet rich and satisfying

Sweet Potato Pancakes

2 eggs, beaten
8 ounces bread crumbs
4 ounces coconut milk
5 1/2 ounces flour
5 sweet potatoes
4 ounces onion, chopped fine
2 3/4 ounces sugar
1 teaspoon crushed red pepper
1 teaspoon cinnamon

Method:

Peel and cook three of the sweet potatoes, mash and set aside, spread out on pan to dry and cool. Peel and shred remaining two potatoes.

Combine all of the ingredients, adding coconut milk last to adjust the consistency. Adjust seasoning to taste. Shape and pan sear the cakes until golden brown.

Crème Fraiche Sauce for Pancakes

1/2 teaspoon cinnamon
1/2 teaspoon nutmeg
1/2 teaspoon allspice
2 teaspoons honey
12 ounces crème fraiche

Method:

Stir cinnamon, nutmeg, allspice and honey into crème fraiche and spoon over pancakes.

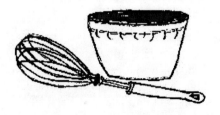

Honey, Pears & Cranberries

16 ounces fresh cranberries
1 quart apple juice
3 pears, peeled, cored, diced
1 cup honey
2 teaspoons vanilla
2 tablespoons unflavored gelatin
1 head Boston Bibb Lettuce

Method:

Bring cranberries, apple juice, pears and honey to a boil in a medium saucepan, then reduce to a simmer until the cranberries pop. Continue cooking until slightly reduced and syrupy.

Meanwhile, dissolve gelatin in about 1/2 cup of warmed apple juice or water.

Remove saucepan from heat and stir in dissolved gelatin. Let cool until slightly thickened, then pour into a serving bowl. Let cool to room temperature. Cover and chill overnight.

Serve over bed of lettuce leaves.

Roasted Pumpkin Soup

1 pumpkin, 6 to 7 pounds
1 1/2 cups herbed bread crumbs, toasted
6 tablespoons butter
2 cups onions, finely chopped
1 cup celery, finely chopped
1 cup carrots, shredded
1 cup Gruyere cheese, grated
1/4 cup Parmesan cheese, grated
4 cups turkey stock
1 cup white wine
1 cup apple juice
1/2 cup heavy cream
1 teaspoon cayenne pepper
2 bay leaves
2 teaspoons nutmeg
Salt and pepper to taste

Method:

Preheat oven to 400 degrees.

With a sharp knife carefully cut a 4-inch diameter opening in the top of the pumpkin. Scrape out the strings and seeds and lightly salt and pepper the interior of the pumpkin. In a heavy skillet melt the butter and cook the onion, celery and carrots until tender but not browned. Stir in the bread crumbs and cook until the butter has been absorbed. Add nutmeg and season to taste with salt and pepper.

Remove pan from heat and stir in cheeses. Spoon this mixture into the pumpkin and pour in the turkey stock, wine and apple juice to within an inch of the rim. Place the bay leaves on top and then put the top back on the pumpkin.

Carefully place the pumpkin in a buttered baking dish and roast for 90 minutes or until the pumpkin starts to soften and the soup is bubbling.

Turn down the oven to 350 and bake another 30 minutes. Cover with foil if the pumpkin begins to brown. The pumpkin should be tender but hold its shape.

When done, remove it from the oven and just before serving, remove the top and stir in the cream. Scrape the sides of the pumpkin to loosen some of the meat, just be careful not to puncture the sides. Eight servings.

Turkey with Curried Currant Sauce

3 pounds turkey tenderloin
2 large onions, finely chopped
2 large carrots, finely chopped
3 stalks of celery, finely chopped
2 sprigs fresh thyme
1 bay leaf
1 cup vegetable stock
1 tablespoon curry powder
1 teaspoon cornstarch
3/4 cup currants plumped in 1 cup white wine
2 tablespoons olive oil
Salt and pepper to taste

Method:

Preheat oven to 350 degrees.

Scatter vegetables in the bottom of a roasting pan, along with the thyme and bay leaf. Coat turkey with olive oil and season with salt and pepper. Place it on top of the vegetables and cover loosely with foil.

Place in oven and bake for 90 minutes or until the juices run clear and a meat thermometer registers 170 degrees.

Remove from oven and let rest for 15 minutes, then slice thinly, reserving the pan contents. Cover turkey and keep warm.

Discard the thyme and bay leaf. Using paper towels, blot up as much of the fat floating on the surface of the liquid in the pan as you can. Using a stick blender (or carefully putting pan contents into a conventional blender) puree vegetables and drippings in the pan. Add combined cornstarch, curry powder and vegetable stock and puree with the pan drippings until smooth.

Put the roasting pan over a burner or transfer the contents of the pan to a small saucepan, add the currants and cook over low heat until thickened and the currants pop. Adjust seasonings to taste.

Wilted Greens & Brown Rice

1 cup brown rice, uncooked
2 2/3 cups vegetable stock
1 tablespoon butter
1 tablespoon canola oil
2 cloves garlic, minced
4 cups fresh spinach leaves
1 tablespoon lemon juice
Salt and pepper to taste

Method:

In a medium saucepan, melt butter over medium-high heat. When it begins to foam, sauté rice until well coated with butter; add stock, stir and bring to a boil. Cover, shut off heat and let sit for 30-45 minutes or until the liquid is absorbed.

To wilt the spinach, heat the canola oil in a large sauté pan and cook the garlic until softened but not browned. Add the spinach and continue stirring until the greens wilt, hit it with the lemon juice and season. To serve put down a bed of spinach, top with rice, then turkey and a ladle of sauce.

Ricotta Torte with Mixed Berries

Crust
1/4 cup oatmeal
3 tablespoons toasted almonds
2 large graham crackers
2 tablespoons light brown sugar
1/4 teaspoon almond extract
2 tablespoons butter

Filling
4 large eggs
2 cups ricotta cheese
3 tablespoons flour
1/3 cup granulated sugar
1 teaspoon vanilla extract
1 tablespoon lemon zest
3 cups fresh or frozen berries (strawberries, raspberries, blackberries, blueberries) whatever is available.

Method:
Preheat the oven to 325 degrees.

Butter a 1-quart soufflé pan.

Using the metal blade in a food processor, finely grind the almonds, add the graham crackers, oats, brown sugar and almond extract and process until well mixed and ground to fine crumbs. Press the crust mixture into the soufflé pan to evenly cover the bottom and sides.

After you wipe out the food processor bowl, combine eggs, ricotta, flour, sugar and vanilla and process until smooth. You can also whisk by hand. Gently fold in lemon zest and carefully pour the mixture into the soufflé pan.

Bake for about 50 minutes or until the batter is set and a toothpick inserted into the center comes out clean. Remove from the oven and let cool for 25 minutes.

To serve, cut into wedges and top with berry mixture.

About the chef ... Doug Janousek

Life is pretty much a journey and while the destination is important, what we do along the way is just as important.

The lessons we take away from every experience shape us for the next one. When I finished culinary school I was asked to give the student address at graduation. What follows is an excerpt of that speech, which actually started out as one of my newspaper columns. So here are 10 life lessons learned (or relearned) at culinary school.

1. Showing up is more than half the battle. That means really being there, professionally attired, groomed, bathed and ready to do what is necessary. That's a pretty big lesson that translates to any job, any position. Some of us, if we're lucky, learned that one early on.

Lesson 2: Wash your hands. Work clean, be clean, be proud of yourself, be confident and professional. It will be reflected in your work.

Lesson 3: Be prepared. Do your homework. Mise en place.

This is a good lesson to apply outside the kitchen and the first place to get organized is in your head – mental mise en place. Once you've got it there, the rest follows.

Lesson 4: Be flexible. Sometimes the best laid plans don't work out. Controlled chaos is the most apt description of what we do. Food orders don't come in, products spoil, someone or several someones don't show up for work ... don't be so rigid that you can't make it through the day.

The mightiest oak tree is likely to fall in the face of hurricane-strength winds, while the willow is able to bend and sway with the forces around it and live another day. Be a willow, not an oak.

Lesson 5: It is all about the technique, baby.

Just as in life, it isn't how big your knife is, but rather how you use it. If you've got the techniques you can apply them anywhere.

Lesson 6: Taste everything. Live it. Be it. Savor it. Drink deeply. Be like Auntie Mame and enjoy life's buffet.

Lesson 7: In the end, it is all about the food. It has to taste good. It has to look good. It has to be consistent. Passion for your cooking means it will taste better, look better and satisfy you better. Apply this to whatever you do. Cooking dinner tonight? Do it with gusto!

When you do what you love, it is easy to put all that passion into it. But sometimes you've got to wash the dishes, sweep the floor, serve the food – and you owe it to yourself, as well as to those who also benefit from your efforts, to do it with the same intensity.

Lesson 8: Put the work in. Do the time. Yeah, the first lesson was to show up, but you know that quality ingredients make quality products. Don't just take up space and oxygen.

Lesson 9: Never stop learning. Learn from your bosses. Learn from your co-workers. Learn from your successes. Learn from your screw ups.

The day I stop learning is the day I can no longer fog the mirror.

Lesson 10: Remember, it is just food. Have fun out there! Life is far too short to do what you don't enjoy.

And here was my big finish: "I don't know about you guys, but this (cooking) is the most fun I've had standing up!"

As you can tell, I had some fun with this speech, just as I do in the kitchen. May your meals be seasoned with the same joy and laughter.

www.home-cookin.net

December

December is the most wonderful time of the year ... decorating the tree, baking the cookies, filling the house with Christmas carols, setting the table with festive drinks, luscious food and gorgeous arrangements to start the magic of the season!

For me, December brings many opportunities to celebrate – the Candles Light Day; my birthday; "novenas," a tradition in my country, Christmas dinner, New Year's Eve and many other occasions give us reason to celebrate the Joy of the Season.

Go ahead and plan to celebrate, decorate, cook, bake, sing and dance. Be with the ones you love and share the joy of giving.

Here is a delicious and different menu that can make your celebration a gourmet experience.

A sparkling cocktail to start, that is so good and flavorful that you can't stop drinking to even to take a breath. A hearty creamy soup that was a result of a happy mistake in the kitchen. The original recipe was for tomatoes with garlic and pearl onions. They were overcooked so it turned into a creamy roasted tomato soup instead.

We think French food is fancy, elaborate and formal, but there are so many kinds of French food.

This pate is just simple, easy and fast to do. You will impress your guests as a gourmet cook!

Continue with the succulent jumbo shrimp seared in extra virgin olive oil, to bring out the exquisite flavor, display them on skewers like a blossoming flower.

There's also an easy and wonderful way to cook asparagus and portobellos, the high temperatures caramelize the outside and leave the inside tender and moist. There's an avocado mousse, with its beautiful color and buttery texture making it a delicacy to indulge your palate.

And to finish this wonderful meal the glorious and magnificent St. Honore', a traditional French cake named for St. Honore, the patron saint of pastry bakers. It is also called "Croquenbouche," French for crisp in the mouth. It is an elaborate dessert but it is worth the time it takes to do it. Assembled in a pyramid shape, with chocolate, decorated with red and green cherries and dusted with powder sugar, it looks just like a little Christmas tree.

– Chef Taty

Holiday Hors D'oeuvres

Sparkling Fruit Cocktail
A delicious blend of pineapple juice, coconut rum and a splash of
coconut cream, garnished with mint and cherries

Cream of Tomato Soup
Roasted tomatoes, peppers and onions, simmered in a creamy chicken
stock, flavored with wine and fresh basil

Dill Shrimp
Succulent jumbo shrimp seared in olive oil, then tossed in a garlic aioli

Pate au Cognac
Chicken livers simmered in butter, cream and spices, flavored with
cognac

Avocado Mousse
Ripe avocados blended with cream, peppers and onions
garnished with cilantro and served with plantain strips

Roasted Portobellos and Asparagus
Marinated in olive oil and spices and
sprinkled with parmesan cheese

Croquenbouche or Saint-Honore'
Pate a choux puffs filled with chantilly cream, drizzled with melted
chocolate and stacked into a pyramid

Sparkling Fruit Cocktail

7 cups pineapple juice
2 cups coconut rum
1/2 cup cream of coconut
3 cups Champagne or other sparkling white wine
Coconut flakes, toasted
Green and red maraschino cherries
Mint leaves
Crushed ice

Method:

The day before carefully place the cherries onto a baking sheet pan and freeze until solid. Toast the coconut flakes in the oven at 350 degrees until light brown.

On the day of serving, combine pineapple juice, coconut rum, cream of coconut and Champagne in a punch bowl, add crushed ice and garnish with frozen cherries, coconut flakes and mint leaves. Ten servings.

Roasted Tomato Soup

6 pounds Roma tomatoes, halved
2 white onions, chopped
6 garlic cloves, crushed
2 carrots, peeled and cut into medium-sized pieces
6 to 8 cups chicken stock
4 tablespoons extra virgin olive oil
3 tablespoons fresh basil, cut in chiffonade
1 teaspoon sugar
1/2 cup heavy cream
Croutons
White wine
Kosher salt and freshly ground pepper

Method:

Preheat oven to 350 degrees. Oil sheet pan with olive oil then place the tomatoes cut side down with the onions, carrots and garlic in a single layer.

Drizzle them with olive oil, salt and pepper. Toss well to coat.

Bake 20 to 25 minutes until the vegetables are very tender, turning once with a spatula. Remove from oven and let cool.

When cool, put them in the food processor and coarsely chop them.

In a large saucepan heat the chicken stock, add roasted vegetables and sugar. Let them simmer for 15 to 20 minutes, then strain the chicken stock and discard the vegetables. Pour the strained stock back into the pot over low heat and season to taste with salt and pepper. Add half of the basil and the cream and let simmer until it gets to a creamy consistency. Serve with the croutons, basil and a drizzle of the white wine. Ten servings.

Dill Shrimp

1 1/2 pounds uncooked large shrimp (25 to 30 count)
Extra virgin olive oil
1 teaspoon garlic, minced
2 tablespoons red onion, finely chopped
1/2 cup mayonnaise
1/3 cup freshly squeezed lemon juice
Kosher salt
Freshly ground black pepper
3 tablespoons chopped fresh dill
1 medium-sized purple cabbage, cut in half horizontally
1 package 8-inch bamboo skewers

Method:

Toss shrimp with olive oil, salt and pepper.

Heat a large sauté pan on high and sauté shrimp just until they turn pink. Set aside to cool.

Add minced garlic and a little bit of olive oil to the mayonnaise. Toss shrimp with onions, lemon juice, dill and the mayonnaise mixture to coat well. Season to taste with salt and pepper.

To serve, place the top half of the cabbage (without the stem), cut side down, on a decorative plate or bowl.

Thread three shrimps onto each 8-inch skewer, bunching the shrimp near the top of the skewer. Insert the skewers into the cabbage so they look like a shrimp bouquet.

Serve leftover mayonnaise on the side as a dipping sauce.

Ten servings.

Pate' au Cognac

1 pound chicken livers, cleaned
4 tablespoons butter at room temperature
1/4 cup heavy cream
4 tablespoons Cognac or brandy
1/8 teaspoon tarragon
Salt and pepper to taste

Method:

In a saucepan melt the butter and add the chicken livers. Let them simmer for about 10 minutes. Add tarragon and season with salt and pepper.

Cook for about 5 minutes longer, then remove from heat.

Transfer to the bowl of a food processor, pulse until smooth.

Add cream, tarragon, salt, pepper and cognac and process until well combined.

Coat the inside of a loaf pan with olive oil and sprinkle the sides with tarragon leaves. Transfer the pate into the loaf pan, smooth the top and cover with plastic wrap.

Refrigerate overnight.

To unmold, dip the pan in warm water for 10 seconds, run a knife around the edge to loosen the pate and unmold upside down onto a flat plate.

Serve with assorted crackers.

Yields 2 cups.

Avocado Mousse

3 ripe avocados, halved, pitted and peeled
1 1/2 cup heavy cream
2 egg whites
2 envelopes of unflavored gelatin
3 tablespoons red bell pepper, finely chopped
2 tablespoon cilantro, finely chopped
Juice of two lemons
1/2 cup of hot water
2 tablespoons cold water
Kosher salt and freshly ground pepper

Method:

In a food processor blend the avocados, lemon juice and cream. Season with salt and pepper.

Beat egg whites until they form stiff peaks.

Dissolve gelatin in 2 tablespoons cold water. When it becomes firm, mix with hot water until it is completely dissolved.

Transfer the avocado mixture to a bowl. Add gelatin, red pepper and cilantro and, using a spatula, very gently fold in egg whites.

Adjust seasoning to taste.

Oil a ring mold and transfer the avocado mixture to it.

Cover with plastic wrap and aluminum foil. Refrigerate over night.

To unmold, dip the ring in warm water for 20 seconds and run a knife around the edge to loosen the mousse. Unmold upside down onto a plate.

Serve with Tostitos or fried plantains strips.

Ten servings.

Roasted Asparagus and Portobellos

2 1/2 pounds fresh asparagus (about 30 large stems)
6 portobello mushrooms
Extra virgin olive oil
Kosher salt and freshly ground pepper
Parmesan cheese shredded
1 cup balsamic vinegar

Method:

Preheat the oven to 400 degrees.

Trim woody ends off the asparagus.

Lay them in a single layer on a sheet pan, drizzle with olive oil and sprinkle with salt and pepper.

Roast for 8 minutes. Sprinkle with Parmesan cheese and return to the oven for 2 minutes. Set aside.

Clean the mushrooms, drizzle with olive oil, add salt and pepper and roast for 10 minutes.

Arrange a platter half with mushrooms and the other half with asparagus.

Make a reduction of balsamic vinegar to serve on the side.

Ten servings.

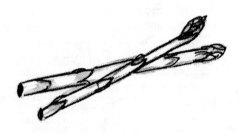

Saint-Honore'

A traditional French cake named for Saint Honore', the patron saint of bakers. Makes about 36 puffs.

1 cup milk
1 cup water
1/2 pound unsalted butter
2 cups all purpose flour
8 large eggs
1 package semi-sweet chocolate chips
1 cup whipping cream
Red and green maraschino cherries for garnish
Confectioner's sugar for dusting

Method:

Preheat oven at 425 degrees.

Line two baking sheet pans with parchment paper. Set aside.

In a medium saucepan, heat milk, water, butter and salt over medium heat until it boils. Remove from the heat.

Add the flour all at once, stir with a wooden spoon until the mixture is smooth and comes together to form a dough.

Cook stirring constantly over low heat for 2 minutes.

Spoon the mixture into a food processor, add the eggs and pulse until the eggs are well incorporated into the dough and the mixture is thick.

Transfer the batter to a pastry bag fitted with a large round tip.

Pipe the dough onto the prepared pans, forming mounds 1 1/2 inches wide and 1 inch high. With a wet finger, lightly press down the top of each puff.

Bake for 20 minutes or until lightly browned, turn off the oven and let them sit for 10 more minutes. Pierce the side of each puff with a skewer to let the steam escape. Set aside to cool. The puffs can be frozen now.

Defrost the day before and leave in the refrigerator until you are going to assemble. Just before assembling inject the whipped cream into the puffs with a ¼-inch pastry tip.

Place the chocolate chips in a bowl set over simmering water and stir just until the chocolate melts.

To assemble, dip the bottoms of the puffs, one by one, into the chocolate and arrange in a pyramid. With a medium pastry tip, fill the spaces between the puffs with whipping cream and place little pieces of green and red cherries on top. Dust with confectioner's sugar. It will look like an edible Christmas tree covered with snow!

About the chef ... Taty Ramirez

When I was just a little girl I asked my mami what I would be. And she said to me, "Always do what makes you happy! That is the key for a wonderful life ..."
And it is true!

I was born and raised in Medellin, Colombia, around a big family that loves to cook, dance and enjoy the good things in life.

I went to design school and after that I went on to study advertising and marketing. While working in the creative department, I fell in love with photography.

As a television and photography director for food products in an advertising agency, my passion for cooking and making food look beautiful brought me into the food styling business. I indulged that passion as a career for more than 20 years, working with photographers and movie directors around the country.

Then I decided to move to the United States and start a new life.

Cooking was my passion and I tried to turn that into a business, but I soon realized that to be successful in the food industry I needed to have a degree. Soon after that, I discovered the Orlando Culinary Academy, Le Cordon Bleu program, where my dreams came true.

With my passion for cooking and experience in food styling, I started this wonderful career by attending classes at night. The night classes were so short to learn everything but I enjoyed so many different things that I can only say I just loved it.

I went to Alaska with my friend Pam, my guardian translator and best companion, to fulfill the externship portion of my education.

That was a great experience! We discovered the first day that instead of doing "mise en place" we have to do Box en Place... convenience food in the end of the world.

I graduated on November 23, 2004, cum laude from Orlando Culinary Academy. I still enjoy my passion as an Executive Chef in a resort and spa in Orlando, FL.

I have a personal chef business serving private parties and cooking for any occasion, special diets and baking the most delicious cookies in the world.

Enjoy my recipes, with all my love.

I can be reached at 407-497-8625 or via e-mail at tatypersonalchef@yahoo.. com.

About the artist ... Anne Jenkins

Anne Jenkins is a British citizen who calls the world home. She was born and raised in South Africa, where she lived for 24 years. She then lived in six European countries for 25 years and traveled the world extensively before settling in the United States. New Orleans was Anne's beloved adopted city for a few

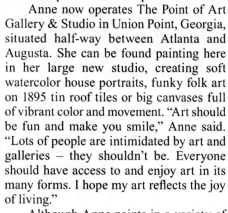

glorious years until Hurricane Katrina blew that part of her life apart.

Anne now operates The Point of Art Gallery & Studio in Union Point, Georgia, situated half-way between Atlanta and Augusta. She can be found painting here in her large new studio, creating soft watercolor house portraits, funky folk art on 1895 tin roof tiles or big canvases full of vibrant color and movement. "Art should be fun and make you smile," Anne said. "Lots of people are intimidated by art and galleries – they shouldn't be. Everyone should have access to and enjoy art in its many forms. I hope my art reflects the joy of living."

Although Anne paints in a variety of media – watercolor, acrylic, pastel – she favors acrylics, using the palette knife technique. This allows her to use thick swathes of paint to create a strong sense of texture.

Her painting of a single sunflower using this technique has been chosen by the state of Georgia as the logo for their brochure, "Georgia Art By the Mile...Heritage Art Loop," a new series of self-guided tours of art and artists in the state.

A self-taught artist, Anne's acrylics and watercolors reside in many private collections in Europe, Canada, and the United States. Among her corporate clients are Universal Studios, Hollywood, California; Datacert Inc., Houston, Texas; and Entergy Power Company, New Orleans, Louisiana.

Anne has worked as a reporter, photographer, banker, English teacher, house cleaner and truck driver. Her travel writing has appeared in such publications as the Los Angeles Times and Opera Now. She and her husband, Lee, spent five years on a sailboat in the Mediterranean; many months in a VW van in Central America, Canada and Alaska; months touring Asia on a shoestring budget; and a couple of crazy years driving a big rig around the Lower 48 and Canada.

Anne's main interests are art, writing, music, travel and good food and wine enjoyed with friends. Her mission statement: To have fun and beat the starving artist rap. She can be found on the Internet at www.ThePointofArt.net and www.annejenkinsart.com.

About the cover: "A Stew of Chefs"

Whenever I browse in bookstores, I always pick up a book if the cover indicates humor and fun. So, I thought – how to make a group of chefs look humorous? Like fun?

I'm not a cartoonist, so the thought of painting a kitchen scene with each chef cooking something was too daunting. It would look way too forced. At first I thought I'd paint a frying pan flat on with the chefs scattered about, but somehow there was too much of that "into the frying pan" cliché. So... if I'm thinking cliché ...what about ... too many cooks spoil the broth? But of course, how ironic! A great cookbook with many cooks *not* spoiling the broth? Oh, yes!

Then it dawned on me. This is a classy bunch of Florida personal chefs, not just restaurants but personal chefs. They ought to be in something akin to the world renowned orange cookware of Le Cruset and it all just fell into place.

I painted Doug in the middle – he's my friend and I think he's the crux of the book. Then the other chefs just "told" me where they wanted to be. The whole painting just flowed after that and sprang to life for me.

I chuckled quite a bit as I painted. I hope you – and the chefs – enjoy it as much as I enjoyed painting it.

Bon appetit!

– Anne Jenkins,
Union Point, Georgia
2006

GALLERY details:

The Point of Art Gallery & Studio
604 Sibley Ave
P.O. Box 202
Union Point, GA 30669
Telephone: (706) 486-6808
www.ThePointofArt.net
Hours: 10 a.m. - 5 p.m. daily except Wednesday and Sunday by appointment.

Meat temperatures

All temperatures are in degrees Fahrenheit. Use an instant-read, digital-type thermometer for accuracy's sake. When checking chicken, make sure the probe is in the thickest part of the meat, not touching the bone. It is best to check more than one spot. In time and with experience, you'll be able to check doneness by the look and feel of the meat.

These recommendations are based on producing the best possible food and are in line with what most people, cooks and diners, traditionally expect as levels of doneness.

However, the United States Department of Agriculture has a slightly different take on the matter, generally recommending higher temperatures, which reduces the potential danger of food-borne illness.

Professional chefs are trained to follow the government guidelines. Those temperatures follow.

Traditional temperatures

Beef

Rare	125
Medium-rare	130-135
Medium	135-140
Medium-well	140-150
Well-done	155 and above

Pork

Once upon a time, pork was cooked well-done and only well done because of the danger of trichinosis and this is ingrained into most home cooks and diners. However, modern pork-producing methods have greatly reduced the dangers of trichinosis.

Cooking pork to medium doneness leaves the meat just lightly pink, but still moist, while getting it well-done is very likely to give you a dry end product.

Temperature where trichinosis is killed	137
Medium	150
Well-done	160

Chicken

Chicken should always be cooked completely done, but just as with other meat, overcooking will make it dry and flavorless (think of some of those Thanksgiving dinners with the really dry white meat).

Breast done	160
Thigh done	165

Lamb

Very rare	125
Rare	130
Medium-rare	135
Medium	140
Medium-well	150
Well-done	160 and above

USDA temperature guidelines:

Beef, veal and lamb

Ground meat	160

Roasts, steaks and chops

Medium-rare	145
Medium	160
Well-done	170

Pork

All cuts

Medium	160
Well-done	170

Poultry

Ground	165
Whole birds	180
Stuffing inside the bird	165
Breasts	170
Thighs	Cook until juices run clear
Egg dishes	160

Measurement conversions

1 pound	16 ounces

Volume measures

1 gallon	4 quarts 8 pints 16 cups 128 ounces
1 quart	2 pints 4 cups 32 ounces
1 pint	1 pound* 2 cups 16 ounces
1 cup	8 ounces 16 tablespoons
1 ounce	2 tablespoons 6 teaspoons
1 tablespoon	3 teaspoons .5 ounce
Dash or pinch	less than ¼ teaspoon

* The old saying is "a pint, a pound, the world round," but that's only partially true. A pint of water weighs a pound, the same goes for milk, but after that it gets more complicated. A pint of denser items, say cream or sugar for example, will weigh more than a pound. Less dense items, like dried herbs, weigh significantly less than a pound when filling a pint measurement.

Most home cooks and the recipes written for them, use volume measurements and recipes turn out just fine.

Professional recipes though, especially those for baking, are often formulated by weight, so converting to volume measure could mean a different end result.

A general rule of thumb is use volume measures unless otherwise indicated.

Another thing to be careful of is doubling recipes. Baking formulas are just that and sometimes it isn't as easy as just multiplying everything times two or three when making larger batches.

That requires a little bit of math, algebra actually – so that guidance counselor in school was right when he or she told you that you would need math later on in life …

So here goes:

1. Determine the percentages of each ingredient to the whole recipe.
2. Determine the new yield and convert that to ounces
3. Dividing the new yield by the total percentage to get the new flour amount in ounces.
4. Multiply the new flour amount (in ounces) by the percentage of each ingredient to get the new amount for each ingredient.

And there you have it. If all the decimals are getting to you and you don't have a digital scale, round to the nearest quarter ounce and you'll be fine.

Metric conversions (approximate)

1 ounce	28 grams
1 pound	500 grams or ½ kilo
2.2 pounds	1 kilo
1 teaspoon	5 milliliters (ml)
1 tablespoon	15 milliliters
1 cup	¼ liter
1 quart	1 liter

Useful substitutions:

1 cup cake flour	=	7/8 cup all-purpose flour plus 1/8 cup cornstarch
1 Tbsp. baking powder	=	2 tsp. baking soda plus 1 tsp. cream of tartar
1 cup buttermilk	=	1 scant cup milk at room Temp plus 1 Tbsp. white Vinegar
1 cup brown sugar	=	1 cup white sugar plus 2 Tbsp. molasses
1 cup sour cream	=	1 cup full-fat yogurt

For more information ...

For more information on personal chefing, visit the editor's Web site at www.home-cookin.net or contact any of the chefs in this book.

To order more copies of **12 Seasons Under the Florida Sun** visit one of these sites:

www.authorhouse.com
www.amazon.com
www.barnesandnoble.com
www.borders.com
www.booksamillion.com

You can also visit your local bookstore and request this title.

Printed in the United States
65255LVS00002B/259-648